JEALOUSY, ENVY, LUST

JEALOUSY, ENVY, LUST

The Weeds of Greed

Richard P. Walters

PYRANEE
BOOKS

Zondervan Publishing House
Grand Rapids, Michigan

Pyranee Books are published by Zondervan Publishing House,
1415 Lake Drive, S.E., Grand Rapids, Michigan 49506.

JEALOUSY, ENVY, LUST
Copyright © 1985 by The Zondervan Corporation
Grand Rapids, Michigan

Library of Congress Cataloging in Publication Data

Walters, Richard P., 1935-
    Jealousy, envy, lust.

    1. Jealousy—Religious aspects—Christianity. 2. Envy—Religious as-
pects—Christianity. 3. Lust—Religious aspects—Christianity. 4. Avarice—
Religious aspects—Christianity. I. Title.
BV4627.J43W35   1985   241'.3   85-3635

ISBN 0-310-42591-3

Unless otherwise indicated, Scripture quotations are from the HOLY
BIBLE: NEW INTERNATIONAL VERSION (North American Edition). Copy-
right © 1978 by the International Bible Society. Used by permission of
Zondervan Bible Publishers.

Edited by Julie Ackerman Link

Printed in the United States of America

85 86 87 88 89 90 91 92 / 10 9 8 7 6 5 4 3 2 1

To those who believe that
"the one who is in you
is greater than
the one who is in the world"
(1 John 4:4)
with the hope that you will
give Him first place
in your life,
always.

Contents

Preface

Good news! God wants to help us change the weak and ugly parts of our lives into strong and beautiful ones. It can happen as surely and as remarkably as it did in any of the unique cases in this book. See for yourself. Seek God with enthusiasm and see dramatic transformations in your life.

The characters in this book are fictional, but the incidents described are based on actual events. They have been altered to disguise persons and places, but the cause-and-effect relationships, the potent role of God's grace, and the changes (startlingly quick in some cases) occurred exactly as described.

Preparing a book requires a lot of help. Thanks to Lorna Devine, Marleen Martin, Terri Anderson, and Anna Janeway for typing; to Ron and Dee Barber for hospitality at Oak Creek Valley, Arizona, where writing began while we were snowed in; to the staff and congregation of First Presbyterian Church, Boulder, Colorado, for support and encouragement; to my many client-friends who have taught me much and whose relationships have enriched this book and my life; to Julie Link, Carol Holquist, and many others at Zondervan Publishing House who have contributed much, giving their best because they, too, wish readers to live in the wholeness that God offers us.

During much of the writing I felt harshly attacked and cunningly distracted by evil. I suspect that each person who seeks to better understand God's truth will have similar experiences. But praise God! Through His grace we are conquerors. When we follow His leadership we emerge from each battle stronger and more aware of His presence in our lives. Christ reigns forever and we with Him. Hallelujah!

1 | Sowing the Seeds

JUNIOR BASCUM WAS AN ENTHUSIASTIC KID— wild, some called him—with a burning urge to get to the Big Time. "Got to unload this last year of high school and move on along," he often said. "This hick town isn't big enough for me."

Foley's Bend was a tired little river-bottom town where mildew hung in the air and Spanish Moss hung on the trees. Once, when Junior had been asked to describe the town, he said that its principle asset was tradition, its leading activity was gossip, and its only usefulness was the occasional export of a talented youth.

"And I'll be the next to go. There's nothing here. Not a job worth having. So I'll go. Me and Debbie Sue— that's my girl—we'll go. Finish the year, get married, and go. Oh, I'm not knocking this place. It's just not for me. The people here are good, but they don't want enough. It's okay for them, but Debbie Sue and me, we want more than we can have here, and we're willing to do whatever it takes to get it. So we're going to go for it. Makes sense, don't you think?"

It was at least familiar. It was the credo of the age: Grab for all the gusto you can get; live and let live, but if anyone stands between you and happiness, move 'em over because you owe it to yourself to look out for Number One.

Junior believed it. His mentor, the media, had subtly taught him that personal pleasure was a noble and achievable goal, and no one had told him otherwise. He even believed there were places where it was always Miller Time, where all the people were Loewenbrau people, and where everyone was a part of the Pepsi generation.

The system broke down for Junior one fall day, but he didn't realize it until a long and painful time later. He had just come out of Mingus Auto Parts and had spotted Debbie Sue leaving Della's Diner, walking in his direction. Debbie Sue wasn't just the prettiest high-school senior in that little town; she would have been the prettiest in almost any town. Junior knew she could be ruthlessly selfish, but when her selfishness was displayed on his behalf he felt wrapped in a protective confidence he found in nothing else.

Junior headed eagerly up the street to meet her just as a black Trans Am glided slowly past. Its heavy-throated pipes rumbled as if to say, "Look at me and eat your heart out." The mirrorlike surface looked as if you could reach right into it as the October sun glistened on the custom metallic-lacquer finish. The chrome wheels flashed as if they were shooting fireworks, and the rolled-leather interior was soft and rich.

The few people on the street stopped walking and pivoted silently in deference to the one-float parade. The driver—cocky, cool behind his mirrored glasses—smirked a bit, pretending to ignore the attention, but counting every head that turned to admire.

Junior saw Debbie Sue stop, her mouth agape. He saw her turn slowly, follow the car, and walk slowly away from him in the direction the car had gone.

"Debbie Sue!"

She was half a block away, walking slowly.

"Debbie Sue!"

No response.

Junior shouted his loudest. "Debbie Sue!"

Her ears heard him, but not her mind; it was imagining what it would be like to ride in that black Trans Am.

Treadwell Brant, who had followed Junior out of the store, touched him on the arm. "Don't worry about it, boy," he said. "Women are funny that way. She'll come back."

Junior felt himself burning—a stinging blush from head to foot—and couldn't look at his friend. "When she does, Tread, she'll wish she was riding with me."

* * *

The world of corporate finance periodically rockets a young genius to the summit. Anthony Bascum had gotten one of those rare rides. Anthony lived 1,682 miles from Junior. No relation, no acquaintance, no connection at all—except he too was afflicted with greed. Like me, like you, like everyone.

He thought he was on top and that he had the trappings to prove the point. He lived in the penthouse of an apartment tower that housed more people than lived in Junior's hometown. He shared this showplace with a cosmetics model whose beauty was so uncommon that it was matched only by the emptiness she felt within. Anthony, caught in the whirlwind of business conquests, knew nothing about that.

He had an executive suite as big as his ego, and he stood in it alone, smirking confidently as he admired the conference table that had just been installed.

Seventy-two square feet of black-walnut surface sparkled at him, and Anthony smugly winked back.

Seventy-two square feet! Bigger than the office he had when he started working here twelve years ago. It was Mallory Forge then, just another small-time, family-owned casting shop. Now it was Bascum Universal—diversified, dynamic, aggressive—and financially things had been very sweet for its leader.

But what jealousy did to Junior Bascum, high-school senior, envy did to Anthony Bascum, corporate wizard. Here's what happened:

Bascum, chief executive officer of a multinational conglomerate, stood amid opulence, surrounded by symbols of his distance above the ordinary. Courted by investors and feared by competitors, elevated to god-man by the serfs of wealth, Anthony Bascum suddenly smelled window screen. Dusty, paint-flecked, rusty, fly-specked window screen.

Anthony scowled. His nose itched. He smelled window screen, and he hated it. *Get out of my life!* he thought. *Out forever! Disappear!* The words roared in his thoughts.

"I left you behind thirty years ago, dirty place! Get out of my life!" He jumped at the sound of his own voice. "I'm talking to myself," he said with disbelief, again aloud. "I'm talking to myself out loud, and I can't help it, and I'm still doing it . . ." His voice trailed off to murmur weakly, "This isn't the way I planned it."

He stood there a moment, almost visibly deflating, before painfully pulling himself together. He rubbed his nose defiantly and stalked solemnly from the room.

He was glad to get to his car. He liked a car door that closed with the precision of a bank vault, and the aroma of leather upholstery was welcome relief. His car, like his office, reassured him of his status; it was a place of refuge. He drove out of the underground garage and into the scramble of traffic, determined to forget, during the short but hectic drive to his water-front apartment, about "that blasted window-screen thing." He knew well enough where the sensation came from, and that was what annoyed him most. It was so long ago, and things were so different now. Why couldn't he shake it?

* * *

Bonnie Bascum and her husband, Don, were living the great American dream with their two children (Didra and Chad), a cat, and a dog in a suburban, four-bedroom, ranch-style house. They lived a long way from Anthony, further from Junior. No relation, no connection.

Bonnie was a Christian, but she had a problem like Junior's and Anthony's. Like me, like you, like everyone, Bonnie was fertile soil for the weeds of greed. The seeds took root one April morning when she attended a seminar at Didra's school to show parents how to enrich their children's education during the summer. It was led by the principal, Toby Forrester, a congenial, intelligent man about Bonnie's age.

Parents in the neighborhood agreed that he was the best principal in the system, and it never sounded corny or excessive when anyone said, "He's devoted to the kids," or "You couldn't ask for a better example for the students."

Toby called Bonnie by name the second time he saw her, and from that moment on she had been captivated by him. It wasn't just his bright, clear eyes, curly hair, or quick and sparkling smile that everyone noticed at first glance. Toby Forrester's attractiveness was based on much more substantial factors than those.

She enjoyed the meeting, made notes with ideas

for the summer, and when the principal invited parents to meet with him personally if they wished to discuss anything, Bonnie quickly made an appointment. The next week she talked with him for twenty minutes about how she could help Didra and Chad.

She was aware of his full attentiveness. He listened carefully to her thoughts and ideas, asked questions to clarify what she meant, and helped her expand on what she said. He obviously cared about her opinion. Bonnie felt as though a valuable possession that had been lost and missing for a long time had been returned. And she was so happy about finding it that she volunteered to be a room mother next year, even though she knew it would put a lot of pressure on her.

As she left Toby's office they shook hands, and he briefly squeezed her arm with his left hand. His touch was gentle; it seemed to radiate warmth deeply, as though she were being touched *through* her arm and not just on the surface. It was not rushed or mechanical, as Don's touch had become. She was sure he had not meant it to be sensual, but . . . ah, she thought, how it could be.

She drove to the grocery store, basking in the affirmation of his parting words: "If every parent had the love for their children you have, this would be a different world." Her arm grew warm as she relived his compliment.

At home, in idle minutes between chores, her thoughts drifted to Toby. She knew he had the kind of commitment to his own family that he praised her for having. She felt some shame as she thought of Don and wondered what he thought about during his long hours of work at the machine shop. Yet, despite shame and fear, her attraction to Toby coaxed her to mellow flute-like tones that were a stark contrast to the creaking and rattling of her relationship with Don, which had come to disrepair through carelessness and neglect.

It was a push-pull week for Bonnie: push away thoughts of Toby; feel the pull again. Hunt for a thread of the magic that once had been the essence of her marriage; feel frustrated. Sense attraction to Toby; feel ashamed. Imagine talking to Don about it; feel afraid. Fantasize about Toby; escape and enjoy.

She asked Don what he thought about when he got bored at the shop. "Oh, nothing," he responded. She told him she wanted to talk about their marriage, and he agreed that it was important, "But not this week, with the bowling tournament coming up." She tried again one night when they were in bed. "I can't talk about that now," he grunted. "I can't listen to you when I need to get to sleep."

Bonnie's mind went to Fantasy Land. She was in Toby's office, and he had been listening to her. He came from behind his desk to thank her for her good idea. He squeezed her arm. Then with a warm, velvet touch, caressed her cheek, and . . .

When Bonnie fell asleep an hour later she tingled all over. But she had to pretend that the stab of shame and the ache of emptiness were not there.

2 | Reaping the Weeds

JEALOUSY, ENVY, AND LUST, the weeds of greed, are old and well established. They are variations of pride, the original sin, and they have grown everywhere throughout the ages.

THE HISTORY

Biblical examples are plentiful, but those that are best known are from the Old Testament. Before the history of man, Satan tried to be more important than God and was evicted from heaven (Isaiah 14:12; Ezekiel 28:12–19). Christ saw him "fall like lightning" (Luke 10:18).

The first generation of mankind, Adam and Eve, followed Satan's sin (Genesis 3) and were evicted from Eden. Likewise, Cain, feeling rejected, envious, and angry because of God's response to his offering, killed his brother and then lied to God, compounding his disobedience. He became "a restless wanderer on the earth" (Genesis 4).

Several generations later, Abram feared the lust of the Egyptians for his beautiful wife, Sarai (Genesis 12:10–20). Envy was rampant, no doubt, as the herdsmen of Abram and Lot quarreled over grass (Genesis 13:7), and wars raged over the lands (Genesis

14). And Sarai was jealous of the pregnant Hagar (Genesis 16).

The sins of pride have roots! And continuity!

When we sin, we're part of an ancient tradition. Jealousy, envy, and lust have been with us from Day One; they flourish in our own hearts, and they will remain with us until that glorious day when God purifies His own. But until then, we need to learn to counteract their subtle attack on our lives and determine how to deal with the problems when they occur in ourselves and in others. First, however, we need to understand, in general terms, why and how they become problems.

THE DEFINITIONS

The word pride covers a lot of territory, but in this book we will narrow our focus to pride that is characterized by excessive or misdirected desire. The word "greed" is a good label for it. Several varieties of greed fit this category. The words used to describe them are used loosely, so each has several definitions that often overlap one another. As a result, the words can be used correctly interchangeably. To avoid some of the confusion this causes, we must sort out the words and agree on definitions before going further.

Desire is the key word here because it is the umbrella under which the others fall. Desire is the longing to acquire something. The object of desire may be tangible: a thing or person; or intangible: a relationship, a personal characteristic, an experience, or a change of circumstances. Usually a desire includes strong feelings and intentions to fulfill the desire.

For example, I desire happiness, joy in family life, to hike in the mountains, world peace, health, to know and enjoy God, to please God, to be cared about, and a car that never needs to be repaired.

Well, okay, the last item is a bit unrealistic. But we all tend to get carried away with our desires. Start your own list, and see if you don't find some that are unrealistic.

I also desire a load of firewood, respect, to never have another pet cat, readers who will forgive me for not wanting another pet cat, lunch, and for the hard things in life to come easily so I won't have to be self-disciplined. . . .

Yes. There I go being unrealistic again. I said it was easy.

I also want socks without holes in the toes, children who have a vibrant Christian faith, and a date with my wife. See how hard it is to keep desires under control?

Oh, yes. I also desire that you have your desires fulfilled . . . but only if your desires don't conflict with mine.

I admit, that's not Christlike, but it's another common human tendency—to elevate ourselves above everyone else. If you listen to yourself this week you might catch yourself at it.

And I desire that all my desires be fulfilled now. Immediately, at the *latest*.

So now you know that I'm greedy, selfish, and impatient. But that's not the worst of it. Sometimes I even desire things that are unquestionably sinful. It starts as temptation, which is not wrong—temptation is disgustingly inconvenient, but not sinful. But it's often hard to throw temptation away. It has appeal, so I give it a place in my mind and think about what it would be like to fulfill it. That's flirting with sin, and it's a very dangerous practice.

Conclusion: Desires are okay, but they are easily contaminated by our sinful nature. Let's define several ways this can happen.

Rebellion: resistance to or defiance of God's

thority. We all desire to control our circumstances, _u_t when this desire is left untended it causes us to resist God and His authority in our lives. Our will becomes as important as God's will.

This is dangerously similar to Adam and Eve's desire for knowledge. When their desire—even though it was a desire for something good—became more important to them than obedience to God, they succumbed to temptation. Satan, the source of all untruth, convinced Eve that she and Adam would know as much as God if they ate the forbidden fruit.

Idolatry: worshiping the wrong object. Idolatry is closely related to rebellion because we allow another object or goal (instead of ourselves or our will) to become more important than God. The object may be appropriate—for example, academic success—but when the desire becomes so strong that it leaves no room for God, it is sin.

Greed: wanting more than enough. Here again, the object may be appropriate—for example, financial security—but the desire is so strong that it competes with our relationship with God and with our ability to fulfill other responsibilities. There are different degrees of greed. For instance, _acquisitiveness_ implies an eagerness to possess and the ability to obtain and keep. It is dangerous behavior because it is moving toward greed. _Grasping_ implies selfishness and often suggests unfair or ruthless means of acquisition. And _avarice_ implies obsessive acquisitiveness, especially of money, and strongly suggests stinginess.

Jealousy: resentment against a rival. Although there are actually two types of jealousy, resentment toward someone who has what you want and resentment toward someone who wants what you have, we will only be concerned with the second, since the first is so similar to envy. Here the object of desire is often appropriate, but there is a perceived rival. This perception triggers the fear of losing the desired object. Such a fear can be healthy and helpful but can easily become excessive. A person with low self-confidence or anyone in a weakly bonded relationship with the desired person is likely to retaliate by taking unhealthy, inappropriate steps to protect the object from the rival. Retaliation of any kind, in thought or deed, is sin.

Covetousness: longing for another's possessions. Here the object of desire is what someone else has. This creates a barrier to relationships, leads to additional sinful behavior, and is clearly forbidden by Scripture.

Envy: covetousness with anger. Anger, often in the form of resentment, is directed toward the owner of the desired object. This resentment is a barrier to relationships, makes retaliation or other sinful actions more likely, and usually leads to the sin of withholding care for one another. In this book we will not make a distinction between covetousness and envy because anger so often is present, and when it is, it must be dealt with clearly and decisively.

Lust: insistent urge toward possession of an object. In general the word *lust* means to have such strong desire to possess something that all else in life becomes less important, a condition essentially the same as described by the words greed and idolatry. In this book, however, we will give attention to the more specific form of lust—that which refers to the mental and physical behaviors when the desire is for the sexual possession of a person. The problem of this kind of lust is twofold: The object is wrong and the intensity is wrong, as will be explained later.

THE SIMILARITIES

From these definitions we see that jealousy, envy, and lust are a lot alike. Each may begin innocently with a legitimate desire. But such a desire, when combined with sinful human nature, can quickly and easily be magnified out of proportion or be directed toward an inappropriate object. Furthermore, our emotions are aggravated by the sinful world in which we live. Society prods legitimate desires to unrealistic levels of expectation and fans the flames of our carnal nature.

In addition, the cluster of feelings associated with jealousy, envy, and lust are strong enough to impede our thinking. When we are highly involved emotionally we cannot think as clearly as when our emotions are at a more moderate level. This makes us vulnerable to temptation and subsequent destructive behavior, which both cause further complications in our lives. For example, when we are jealous of another person our resentment may lead us to hurt him or her in some way. This, of course, is likely to provoke a counter-attack, which makes us want to increase our retaliation. And on it goes.

THE CONSEQUENCES

Allowing the weeds of greed to grow uncontrolled in our lives has both social and spiritual consequences. Resentment, frustration, fear, guilt, and shame are just a few of the painful emotions that are the consequences of jealousy, envy, and lust. These are likely to cause conflicts with others, often in the form of overcompetitiveness, scheming, withholding co-operation, and a general breakdown of trust and community, and they often lead to additional sins, such as lying, stealing, or sexual immorality.

The spiritual consequences of jealousy, envy, and lust are even more serious. Since our behavior is condemned by God, it creates a barrier between us and Him. And as long as we insist on clinging to our sinful behavior, we give up any chance of improving our relationship with Him. When we neglect this relationship, we lose our spiritual armor and are wounded unnecessarily and excessively by the ever-present "darts" of the enemy.

THE PRICE

Although out-of-control desires are part of normal human experience, a consequence of our sinful nature, they must be controlled because of their tremendous potential for destruction. And although controlling them is extremely difficult, praise the Lord it's not impossible!

Mankind continues to make the mistake that Adam and Eve made. We recognize our mortality and our vulnerability in the face of a thousand and one hazards in our environment and we are afraid. We try to cope with the fear by gaining control. We believe that by being in control we will not be afraid. To try to get control we defy God's laws. We eat forbidden fruit.

We chomp, we nibble, we gulp the forbidden fruit.

It doesn't satisfy, but we learn so slowly. In frustration we redouble our efforts, but make the same mistakes. Chomp, nibble, gulp.

God gives us laws to make our lives easier. He wants to teach us how to live successfully. But we don't want to be submissive; we want to be His equal. So we live by a system based on Satan's deception—a system that won't work because evil has consequences that cannot be avoided.

We learn the hard way that the forbidden fruit is actually poisonous.

There is always a price to be paid for sin, and it is paid out of the most valuable asset we have—the one commodity that cannot be replenished—time. The price of sin is living without the fullness of God within us, settling for survival, not life.

My desire for you is that this book will help you achieve wholeness and joy. Please join me in praying toward that end:

> Gracious Lord, teach me what I need to learn about my thoughts and deeds that distance me from you. Show me the jealousy, envy, and lust in my life. Make me uncomfortable with these sins. Give me strength and honesty to welcome the spotlight of your truth into the dirty corners of my life, so that I can become more complete and be more like my Savior, your Son, Jesus Christ, in whose name I pray.

Jealousy

3 | A Gardener's Guide to Jealousy

JEALOUSY IS THE RESPONSE WE MAKE when we fear that we will lose an object we desire. It is a painful cluster of feelings—fear, anger, shame, sorrow—and it often leads to thinking and behavior that is wrong and that adds to the discomfort.

The object of desire may be appropriate—another person and their caring for us—but the jealous response may lead to thinking and behavior that are anything but appropriate. Responses such as suspiciousness, retaliation to the threatening person, and manipulation of other people are common. They are usually disruptive and often become sinful without our awareness. If it is an inappropriate desire, e.g., to receive adulation from another person's spouse, or if the level of desire is excessive, the problems are multiplied.

It's agonizing.

So, let's learn how to keep jealousy from becoming a problem for us.

SEED

Jealousy (as we defined it in chapter 2) sprouts from the fear of losing something important to us, which is a normal response when something we value is threatened. A certain level of fear is proper and healthy because it causes us to protect and prudently care for what we have. The essential element in jealousy, the element that distinguishes it from a healthy response, is an overexaggerated fear of losing. The belief that "I'm going to lose," even though there may be no basis for such a belief, is likely to cause a very strong emotional reaction.

SOIL

Inferiority is the primary internal condition that makes it easy for the seeds of jealousy to sprout. Those who believe they "can't compete" are likely to have a great deal of fear. They tell themselves over and over again that they have little to give and that other people are better than they are. Eventually they begin to wonder what anyone else could see in them. Believing themselves to be inferior and bombarding themselves with self-doubt, they will likely develop a strong sense that one or more areas of life are out of control. In such conditions the seeds of jealousy can easily sprout.

Although *believing* that one is not in control of life can cause jealousy, jealousy is even more likely to sprout if part of life is in reality out of control.

SURROUNDINGS

External conditions are also a factor. One external factor that affects jealousy is the progress we are making toward the fulfillment of legitimate desires. A lack of progress can lead to jealousy. The person who is not getting enough total satisfaction in life is likely to become protective and possessive about every portion of life that is satisfactory.

The threats and problems may be real, but we must deal with them constructively so we don't destroy ourselves with jealousy.

SUN AND WATER

Even when the conditions are right for the seed of jealousy to sprout, we don't have to nurture it by providing the sun and water that allow it to come to life.

Overvigilance is an important source of nourishment for jealousy. When we demand that every act of the object-person be accounted for, we put ourselves in a "detective" relationship that is always unhealthy. Any ambiguous or partly understood behavior of the object-person becomes suspect, and when we assume the person is guilty, we are likely to interpret every act in the worst way. From there it is just a short step to exaggerating the consequences of what could happen.

Overidentification with another person also nourishes jealousy. Some people fail to see themselves as unique and independent; they operate as though they are just an extension of another person. This kind of person is likely to be jealous if there is the slightest threat to his or her relationship with the desired person. Overidentification is common behavior for anyone who feels inferior, because identifying with someone stronger gives a temporary sense of control and power.

Polly was that way. When I asked her who she was, she replied, "I'm Jim's wife." That was all. She could not describe anything about herself in terms other than her role as Jim's wife.

"Who are you, Polly?"

"I'm Jim's wife."

She not only loved Jim, she *was* Jim. Consequently she wanted to know everything that was going on in his life. She worried about what he was doing when he was at work, when he was traveling to and from work, when he was with his bowling team, and so on. And on and on.

Because Polly believed she would no longer exist if

she were not Jim's wife, she needed a lot of proof that her status as his wife was not in jeopardy. She began to play detective, and because she assumed she had nothing worthwhile to give and could not compete with other women, she got caught up in worrying. She began making unfounded interpretations of Jim's behavior, following him around, spying on him, and badgering him for details. Jim finally felt as if he were being driven out of the marriage. Suddenly, Polly was no longer Jim's wife.

Unfaithfulness also nourishes jealousy. It's wrong in itself, of course, and it introduces jealousy because those who are guilty project their behavior to others and assume others are equally guilty.

THORNS

The weeds of greed grow no tasty fruit; they grow only thorns that savagely wound those who come near. Brer Rabbit may have preferred the briar patch, but you and your friends won't. Let us look at four kinds of thorns.

Mental/Emotional. Jealousy causes unhappiness. It arises out of fear, and it grows more fear. It also grows depression, nervousness, hurt, anger, suspiciousness, mistrust, and loneliness.

Physical. When jealousy is buried within, it increases stress-related illnesses. These may include ulcers, colitis, twitching, general muscular tension, and others. Jealousy even has an effect on the face because tension causes worry furrows on the brow and along the mouth, hardness of lips, and perhaps clenching or grinding of teeth.

Relational. Suspiciousness and mistrust cause broken relationships because these behaviors make the jealous person less attractive. Consequently, people avoid the jealous person, which is likely to confirm the suspiciousness. Possessiveness is also a common protective behavior. One jealous woman would not let her husband watch certain television programs because of the attractive women they featured. His solution was to go to a friend's house to watch the programs. Her possessiveness backfired.

Efforts to get attention, even when they are honest cries for help, are likely to be ineffective because they are indirect and unrecognizable. A jealous middle-aged woman suddenly began wearing provocative teen-styled clothing. Instead of developing inner beauty, she was trying to compete physically with other women. Her husband was embarrassed and angry. She looked worse to him, not better.

Jealousy breeds hatred and spite, and these usually lead to attempts to hurt the rival. A man who was jealous of a business competitor bid against him on a construction job. The jealous man submitted such a low bid, to prevent his rival from getting the job, that it led to his own bankruptcy. More often, jealousy leads to lack of cooperation, spreading gossip, verbal abuse, or physical violence.

Spiritual. Jealousy diverts us from our relationship with God. It grows, crowding out healthier, more useful activities and thoughts. It can lead us into attitudes and behavior that are wrong.

The thorns of jealousy are deadly. We will be wounded often enough by the thorns of others; we don't need to grow any of our own.

CHOPPING IT BACK

The following techniques will help us cope with jealousy. Coping, however, is only a place to begin; it is not the final solution. But by learning to cope we can keep the problem under control as we prepare to eliminate it altogether.

Pray. Jealousy is a sin, and Satan uses it to

destroy us. We need God's help to deal with it, and God's help is readily available.

Do not condemn yourself. This only makes matters worse by adding to the inferiority you may already feel.

Put things into perspective. The Christian is to live by faith, not by mood. Perhaps you are afraid. Of what? What are the facts?

Think of the consequences. If you allowed jealousy to run rampant, what would happen? Have a healthy respect for the destructiveness of jealousy, but, I remind you, don't condemn yourself if you're struggling with the problem.

Keep busy. Interesting daily activities will leave no room in your life for jealousy.

Counteract thoughts of suspicion. By filling your mind with that which is good and wholesome you can crowd out harmful thoughts.

Understand the other person better. Perhaps you will be more motivated to do this if you remind yourself of your responsibility as a representative of Christ to that person.

Admit your jealousy. This step is essential to healing. You cannot deal effectively with a problem while pretending it does not exist.

Enlist help. Ask a trusted friend to support all of your thinking and behavior that is healthy and to confront you about any thinking or behavior that is unhealthy.

Take control. Remind yourself of the power and control available to you. We are created in God's image and have tremendous capacities for constructive thinking and action. You probably are living effectively in many areas of your life. Celebrate that.

Imagine the worst. Reevaluate the importance of the desired object. Is it actually as important as you think it is? If the threat is real, perhaps you will lose the object. How bad would that be?

Imagine the best. Perhaps the rival dislikes your desired object. Or perhaps the object is not as important to the rival as you believe it is.

Reward yourself for coping. If you have used even a few of these suggestions, you have taken constructive action and should be praised and rewarded. Think of some creative way to reward yourself.

DIGGING OUT THE ROOTS

The roots of jealousy go deep, so the process of destroying them may be painful. Before we can have relief from jealousy's choking vines, however, we must get to the root of the problem. Several tools are necessary to complete this job effectively.

Honesty. If you have not already admitted to yourself that you have a problem with jealousy, do so now. You cannot offer a true confession to God if you have not admitted your problem.

Confession and repentance. Ask God to reveal sinful attitudes and behaviors and then confess each one and deal properly with it. This may involve apologizing for reactive or protective acts committed when jealous. Remorse is not enough; repentance includes an honest intention to behave differently in the future. If we confess and repent, God will heal us of the internal conditions that made us vulnerable to jealousy. He will also help us become strong enough to resist the temptations of external circumstances. But this is a long-term process; confession and repentance do not make us immediately immune to temptation.

Self-understanding. Since we tend to see our own faults magnified in others, perhaps you are guilty of doing some of the same things the other person did that made you jealous. Ask God to make you aware of your own behavior that you may be projecting onto another and to teach you what you need to learn about yourself in this situation. Taking action to correct these faults will help resolve the jealousy.

Problem clarification. In addition to understanding yourself, it is important to understand the origin of the problem. Talk about it with someone who is well informed, perhaps a trusted friend, a minister, or a Christian counselor. When you begin to understand why you respond the way you do, you will begin to see ways in which you can grow and develop as a person. Ask God to provide the resources—friends, teachers, supporters—that will help you in those areas.

Polly, for example, needed to relearn some mistaken ideas about herself that she had learned early in childhood. Her relationship with her mother had been exactly like her relationship with Jim. She had failed to develop a sense of personal identity. Also, she had not learned some of the important skills of assertive living; consequently, she felt threatened much more often than necessary.

KEEPING FREE

Maintaining a proper lifestyle is important so that when jealousy sprouts again, as it is likely to, it will not find conditions that make it easy for it to grow.

Develop a strong devotional life. The joy of life in Christ is one of the most effective deterrents to sinful habits.

Develop virtuous qualities. This will help you like yourself more, and a positive self-concept will help alleviate a major cause of jealousy—the fear that something valuable will be lost to a rival.

Ask for help. Don't baby yourself, but while you are growing stronger, it may be proper to ask other persons in your life, especially a spouse, to moderate his or her behavior so that it does not exceed your threat level.

4 | Junior Gets in the Driver's Seat

THE MORNING AFTER THE TRANS AM drove through Foley's Bend, Debbie Sue found a quickly scribbled letter from Junior inside her screen door as she left for school.

"Debbie Sue: I got tired of waiting for spring. I can find better things to do than sit around this place waiting to graduate. By the time school's out things will be a lot different. Just see if they aren't. Don't do anything silly, like get married, before you see me again. That might not be for a few months because some pretty big things are going to happen. Don't miss out. Take care. I love you. Junior."

Junior's mother didn't have any more information. "He left real early this morning, Debbie Sue. I think he must have been up all night. He got his things together and just left; that's all. He didn't seem mad about anything, but he sure did seem determined. He promised to write. He didn't know where he was going; just said he was going to find a job where he could earn some money and earn it fast. He talked about Mobile and New Orleans and even the oil fields . . . oh, I hope he doesn't do that."

"He's big and strong, and he has good sense, Mrs. Bascum. Junior will be all right."

"He'll be all right, but I wish he was here with us."

A week later Mrs. Bascum got a post card from Pascagoula where Junior was working in a convenience store. Later a letter came saying, "I'm a roustabout on an off-shore oil rig. The pay and the food are good." There was a Christmas card postmarked New Orleans, and as the southern winter merged into a slowly unfolding spring, a post card came from Houston, and at Easter time a letter. These didn't explain much but hinted that Junior would be back in Foley's Bend soon.

The last week of school Debbie Sue got a post card that said, "Watch for a U.F.O. coming in on Highway 83." The morning of graduation day Junior arrived driving a new Corvette, showroom clean, opalescent finish that enveloped him in a bright rainbow bubble. Junior was dressed in expensive, casual clothes, from the gold chain around his neck that highlighted his deeply tanned face to the toes of his hand-tooled boots. Debbie Sue couldn't believe how good he looked, couldn't believe the car, couldn't believe it was paid for, couldn't believe the roll of bills Junior casually displayed. She couldn't believe it, but she did like it! It was like a dream come true.

"They told me it couldn't be done," Junior said, and Debbie Sue didn't notice the frightened edge in his voice. "Whatever you've been planning for the next six months, forget it all. We're getting married this weekend." And they were.

Now, eight years later, they were living in a tract home in a suburb of New Orleans. The Corvette had been replaced by a pair of small cars. Junior was manager of an electronics store, taking courses whenever he could and working toward owning a computer store. Debbie Sue had become a licensed dental assistant and was working in a nearby clinic.

The cars were rather old because Junior was saving all their money to invest in their own business.

They had a pretty good start already. Where all the money they had when they first got married had come from, Debbie Sue didn't know. Some question marks hovered over the marriage.

Junior's time away from Foley's Bend was a taboo topic. "It was boring," he said, "just work, work, work."

There were other fragments. Though nothing by themselves, they accumulated to make Debbie Sue uneasy. For example, a liquor store across the street from the dental clinic was held up one afternoon as Debbie Sue was leaving work, and she saw the owner shoot at the fleeing robber. "How could anybody have the nerve to do anything like stick up a store?" she said to Junior later that evening as she told him the story.

"I can understand that," he replied. "When you know what you want, if you really want it, you do what it takes. You figure what the risks are; you plan how to take care of the risks; and you go for it. I can understand that."

There was also a time when he seemed to know more than he should about drug traffic. But he glared at her when she asked him how he knew so much, so she didn't ask that question again.

As long as Debbie Sue catered to Junior's demands things went smoothly. "When a man knows what he wants, like Junior does," she said to a friend, "you give him plenty of leeway. I can look out for myself, and I can push on people when I have to, but I have learned that you don't do that with Junior."

They were both busy, doing well in their work, and, for a pair of desperately ambitious people, surprisingly tranquil. Until a warm Tuesday evening.

"Junior, there's a Dental Society banquet this weekend. Dr. Walsh is getting some kind of honor, and he wants everybody in the office to go. He wants to pick me up and take me there."

"The guy isn't married, and you are, and he thinks he's going to take you out?" Junior exploded. "The guy's out of his gourd!"

"It's not 'taking me out!' It's some kind of dumb, stuffy professional banquet; that's all. We just go there, and then we come back; that's all. He considers it part of my work. He's paying me for it, even."

Her words were lost on Junior; fear and anger had closed his ears to her explanation. "This guy with the fancy first name, this Bennington Walsh, D.D.S., who probably powders his face and sleeps in lace pajamas, can rinse and spit himself right out of my life! Tell him if his Mercedes shows up in my driveway, there better be an ambulance right behind it, 'cause he'll be in no shape to drive when he leaves."

Debbie Sue was pale, trembling, bewildered. Junior had always been strong-minded and domineering, and he had been loud before, but she had never seen anything like the fury of this outburst.

Junior stood holding a rolled-up newspaper. "Nobody touches my wife!" he screamed, slapping the newspaper on the palm of his hand. "Nobody even thinks about it! Not this two-bit mouth mechanic; not anybody! You can quit that job first, you hear? You can quit, but you can't go out with the guy; you got that?"

Debbie Sue got it, but she didn't know what to do with it. She knew the depth of her commitment to Junior made his fears groundless; his reaction came from a source she didn't understand. It would be futile to try to talk further with him about it, but she had already decided to go to the banquet Saturday night. Frightened and confused, yet struggling, she simply and quietly said, "I got it."

Saturday afternoon Debbie Sue announced that it was time for her to get ready to go to the Dental Society dinner. Junior looked at her with laser-beam intensity and silently left the house. He drove to a part of town where he knew there would be women waiting on the sidewalk to invite him upstairs. When he came back home the next morning his money and self-respect were gone, but his anger wasn't; it was beating on him instead of Debbie Sue.

Debbie Sue was propped up in bed when Junior entered. As she started toward him he said roughly, "Don't even think about touching me."

"I love you, Junior. I've been worried."

"Just get out of my way." He moved clumsily toward the bed and fell on it face down. "Just go away."

She left the room, quietly closing the door behind her, and lay down, exhausted and worried, on the living-room sofa. Through the long, fitful morning she heard Junior thrashing in his sleep, heard him curse himself, and heard him crying. Her own experience was similar.

In midafternoon she heard Junior in the shower and realized she had been sleeping well for a couple of hours. When he finished his shower she went into the bedroom hoping to talk with him. "Junior, I'm sorry. I shouldn't . . ."

"You should have been sorry yesterday. I gave you a direct order not to go out with that man."

She felt her anger rising. "I didn't 'go out with him.' All it was, was that I went to a dumb dinner. It was boring, and I didn't have a good time, and I was back here by 8:30."

"After I told you not to go!"

"It was part of my job. I had to go."

"What you have to do is be my wife," Junior shouted. "Who's in charge here, you or me? And who's the man in your life, me or him?"

"You don't need to ask that. You know I love you,

Junior. I always have. Why can't things be like they used to be?"

"Because you disobeyed. Now, you answer me a question: If you had it to do over again, would you go?"

Debbie Sue wanted to explain to Junior that it wasn't a matter of who was right, but of choosing to work it out or not to work it out. She wasn't willing to lie and say no, but she was frightened to the core to tell the truth. She said what she had to say, "Yes."

She had the kind of "lifetime in a split second" experience that she thought was merely a contrivance of the movie industry. She saw Junior's hand pull back as if in slow motion, then hurtle palm forward toward her face, gathering momentum every inch, closer, closer, hurtling so fast, and yet it seemed so long before she heard the explosive slap of his hand against her head, palm against cheekbone, and felt a shock wave smash through her. Her knees buckled, and she crumpled at his feet. She looked up at Junior's livid, scowling face, and it seemed miles away. "Get out!" she heard him demand in a deep, acid-edged hiss.

She fumbled to her feet, groped through tears for her purse as she passed through the living room, and almost blindly stumbled outside to the car. Head throbbing, heartsick, gasping for breath, and trembling, she got the car started and drove aimlessly for a couple of hours, only dimly aware that she was honked at occasionally. She finally stopped in a park and slumped over in the seat sobbing. It was dusk when she decided to go home.

She entered cautiously. Junior was propped in the corner of the sofa, his lap and the cushions covered with snapshots.

Debbie Sue spoke hesitantly, "I've just come to get a few things. I won't be but a minute."

Junior burst into tears. He looked old, haggard,

exhausted, but it was a little boy's voice that pleaded, "Don't go. Please, don't go." He stood, pictures of happier days cascading from his lap, arms outstretched. "Don't go."

She rushed to him. They embraced, both convulsed with fear and pain. They cried for different reasons, but they cried as one.

"I'm crazy," Junior said. "I'm crazy from jealousy. I'm crazy from things I've done. You're all I've ever cared about, but I've ruined it all. Don't let me ruin it. Help me figure out what to do. I'll do whatever it is."

It was a long time before the roots of jealousy in Junior's life were dealt with. It began that evening when they decided to work on it together. It wouldn't have happened without that, nor is it likely that it could have happened if they had not accepted a personal relationship with God.

Through counseling, Junior began to understand the connection between his jealousy and the deep sense of abandonment he felt when his father deserted the family during Junior's childhood. Junior also learned that trying to build a relationship with Debbie Sue by dazzling her with money, as he did at the time they got married, or by enforcing dictatorial demands, as he had tried more recently, was futile.

In addition to confessing and repenting to God, Junior did what he could to make restitution for crimes he had committed before marrying Debbie Sue. Although he was not prosecuted for these, he made restitution out of his savings earmarked for the new store. As an economy move they sold both cars, but they remained optimistic about saving enough money to buy at least a share of a store of their own. They agreed that the sacrifices didn't matter because they had found inner peace; and because they knew they were in it together, it was easier to be patient.

The day they sold the second car Junior and

Debbie Sue boarded a city bus. "I never rode a city bus before," Debbie Sue said.

"Neither have I," said Junior, "but you know something funny? Now that I'm getting my act together, for the first time in my life I feel like I'm in the driver's seat!"

5 | Alex Learns to Help a Jealous Spouse

ALEX HASKINS WHEELED HIS TRUCK into the driveway, happy to be home at the end of a hard week. Marni met him at the door, frowning, her dark eyes narrowed.

"Where have you been? You should have been here half an hour ago." There was accusation in her voice.

Alex's joy disappeared. "Don't start in on me!"

"It's a reasonable question."

"And I said, 'Don't start in on me!'"

"I'm not starting anything. I'm just interested in your life, that's all. What kind of wife would I be if I wasn't interested in you?"

"Oh, come off it. All you want to do is play your silly detective game. I'm in no mood for it!"

"And I'm supposed to feel sorry for you, installing telephones in offices all day long with all those pretty secretaries hanging around you. I'm supposed to feel sorry about that! And if I worry because you don't get home on time, then according to you there's something wrong with *me*. I'm in no mood for *that!*"

"Look, I've been working hard all week. I'm tired; I'm hungry; I want some peace and quiet. After all I've been through this week I think I deserve that."

"You must think I haven't been doing anything all week. I cook for you. I wash your clothes. I take care of the house. I take care of the kids. And the kids have been terrible this week. And while I'm doing all that . . ."

"While you're doing that, I'm working even harder."

"Don't interrupt me! You don't even care enough about me to listen to my side of it!"

"Sure I do, but I've heard it all before—all your self-pity, all your suspicions, all your accusations. I don't need it, woman."

"Woman!" Marni exploded. "Woman! That's all I am, huh? Woman. You don't love me anymore, do you?" She walked quickly toward the bedroom. "You just don't want me anymore, do you?" It wasn't a question; it was an accusation.

She slammed the bedroom door behind her. Alex stood just inside the front door where he had entered. He stared at the floor, slowly shaking his head. He moved haltingly to the couch and sat down, feeling bewildered and helpless.

He pictured her sprawled across the bed, sobbing, and he felt tears in his eyes on behalf of the self-doubt and fear that he knew were very real to her. At the same time he felt anger welling up inside him from the frustration of this episode; it was painfully similar to dozens that had preceded it.

Alex knew he was becoming indifferent to her, and he was afraid. He didn't like it, but she had pushed away every attempt he made to change the pattern that was driving them apart. He wanted counseling for both of them, but she screamed a refusal at him when he suggested it. He buried his face in his strong hands, massaging his tightly closed eyes as if polishing a crystal ball that would tell him what to do. No answer came.

A month later on a Wednesday evening, Alex slowly turned his truck into the driveway and shut off the ignition. He sat tensely, mentally reviewing the suggestions given him by the counselor he had talked with three times during the last two weeks. After rehearsing his plan, he walked cautiously toward the front door.

Marni's greeting was lukewarm. "You're home in good time tonight."

"Traffic was light. How were you and the kids today?"

"Okay. Mostly, anyway. How was your day? Where were you working?"

"It was a good day. Rewired some things at the university this afternoon; I may be there the rest of the week. What did you mean when you said, 'Okay, mostly?' Did the kids give you some problems?"

"At the university, huh? All kinds of beautiful legs walking around over there! I'll bet you enjoyed that! Where were you, in the girls' dormitory?"

"I was rewiring a panel in a utility closet in the biology building. I was looking at wire and terminals all day."

"That's what you tell me."

"Yes. Because that's the way it was. I'm interested in how your day was and something you said makes me think that maybe it wasn't an easy day for you. I'd like to hear how it went and if you need my help with anything."

Marni spoke sarcastically. "Oh, sure. You spent the day with your eyes bugged out looking at all those foxy young things prancing around over there, so why would you want to come home and have anything to do with me?"

"I said all there is to say about how I spent my day. So I'll tell you what's important to me right now. I'm interested in what's going on in your life. Because I love you."

"If you love me so much, why don't you answer my questions?"

"I'll answer every question that's a worthwhile question. Like I said, I've already told you everything worth saying about what I did today. When you keep asking questions, it makes me feel like I'm being accused of something. It bugs me."

"It wouldn't bug you if you didn't have something to hide."

"That's not why it bugs me. It bugs me because it's not good for you. It's not good for our life together."

"You must be trying to hide something."

Alex was silent. His mind raced through the conversations he had had with his counselor and then went through his mental list of strategies they had discussed. He decided to not say anything.

"You won't deny it," Marni said triumphantly.

"I've told you everything there is to say. There isn't anything more about my day to tell you. I think I'll change my clothes."

Alex went to the bedroom. As he sat on the edge of the bed he reviewed the suggestions he had been trying to follow:

Refuse to reinforce jealousy-related interrogation. As frustrated as Alex was he chuckled when he thought about what his counselor had said: "Interrogation will do as much to quench jealousy as eating a bowl of dust will do to quench thirst." The counselor suggested that Alex give one or two reasonable replies; if those explanations were not accepted he should be silent or leave the room.

Show interest in the jealous person, but on healthy terms. Listen for leads that could open the door to discussions about things that are important to the jealous person but are not part of the interrogation. Alex had tried to pick up on Marni's comment that her day had been "Okay, mostly."

Reassure the jealous person of his or her intrinsic worth. Their behavior might be immature or sinful, but they still have personal value.

Reassure spouse about commitment to the marriage.

Report the effect that the interrogation has on you.

Alex decided he had done reasonably well. He had used each of these strategies to some extent. He knew he couldn't change Marni, but he would be responsible for his behavior. He would not encourage her problem and maybe he could make her want to change. He gave himself a *B−* on his efforts.

When Alex arrived home the next night he was a bit more confident than he had been on Wednesday. He again reviewed his plan and prayed before going into the house.

"Have a nice day at the girlie farm, Alex?"

"I had a busy day at the university chasing wires through the basement of the biology building," Alex replied casually.

"How many pretty girls did you look at?"

"None, Marni."

"Ha!"

"Marni, it really hurts me when you go on like this. It's not good for us . . ."

"Tell me about everyone you talked to today."

"No, because that's trivial, and it's not good for either of us when you quiz me like this. I will tell you what is worth telling you, but I'm not going to go along with this third-degree, rubber-hose interrogation treatment you give me."

Marni burst into tears. "You don't love me."

"Marni, I do. I'm glad we're married. I married you because I like the way you look, because we believe the same way about important things, because we have so much fun together. But something's spoiling that now. I don't know why all these questions are so important to you, but they're driving us apart. I'm not blaming you for all this, but together we need to change it. It's a problem that belongs to both of us, because whatever it is, we both end up feeling bad."

Marni sat down at the table and laid her head on

her arms. Alex wasn't sure if she was crying or listening, but he went on. "Marni, I have really wanted to find out how I could be a better husband. I haven't wanted to make difficulties for you. So, for the last couple weeks I have been talking to a counselor to find out how I could be a better husband."

Marni sobbed. Alex stood beside her, his hand massaging her shoulder. "I'll do whatever I can to help this marriage be a better one. I'd like your help with that. The counselor says he can understand me better if he gets to know you better, too. Will you come with me to the next appointment?"

There was a long silence. Marni muttered, "There's nothing wrong with me."

"But there's something wrong with our marriage, Marni. Let's do everything we can to figure it out." He pulled a chair close to hers and sat down with his arm around her shoulders. They sat silently for quite a while.

Alex had again refused to reinforce the interrogation, had reaffirmed his commitment to the marriage, and had affirmed Marni. In addition, he had implemented three more of the counselor's suggestions:

State that you will not, in the future, reinforce jealousy-related interrogation.

Help the jealous person understand that a problem exists. Don't pity the person bound by jealousy but include educational information about jealousy in the conversation. This will not have a dramatic, immediate effect, but it may begin to build an awareness that some things need to change.

Ask the jealous person to attend counseling with you. Jealous people are more likely to take part in counseling if their role is to give information about someone else. Because jealousy causes such a high level of suspicion and defensiveness, those who are jealous are not as likely to attend if they feel they will be targeted as the person with the problem. It is nearly always necessary for the "healthier" spouse to take most of the blame at the beginning.

Alex gave himself an *A* for effort and a *B* for performance. When Marni said "Okay, if you want me to go, I suppose I'll go," he silently rejoiced.

Marni was somewhat annoyed after their appointment with the counselor.

"He talked to me way more than he talked to you. You're the client, not me. And it seems like he's expecting me to do all the changing."

"Yeah, maybe it did seem that way," Alex laughed. "But you ought to hear him jump on me. Believe me, he's already pointed out lots of things about me that need to change. And I'm trying to change them."

"Such as?"

"Not hiding in front of the TV set or by working on the car or going bowling or even doing too much of some worthwhile things like Little League coaching or volunteer work at church. I'm trying to enter into your life much more now."

"I like that," Marni said and reached for his hand. They sat quietly, smiling.

Marni soon began to attend the counseling sessions regularly. The counselor had explained some other things to Alex that helped him understand and help Marni.

The spouse of a jealous person has an important role to play. The spouse should not do things—for example, flirt—that hurt the jealous person. Alex was glad he had not followed the advice of a friend who had told him the way to fight jealousy was to "go ahead and do what she is accusing you of doing. Then she'll shape up." Alex had been so desperate that the suggestion had some appeal when he first heard it. He realized now that following his friend's advice would not only have been wrong but that it would have been detrimental and counterproductive.

Only the jealous person can change himself or herself.

A jealous person needs a program of personal healing and development. This is almost certain to be a time-consuming, long-term project and should be aided by a competent professional. Marni became involved in this way and came to understand the underlying causes of her jealousy, became free of the fears on which it was based, and developed a healthy sense of self-worth. The marriage prospered.

Alex bounded into the house on a Friday afternoon ten months later. "I was in the biology building at the university today. I hadn't been there for almost a year. It got me thinking about some things."

Marni laughed. "Like my imaginary competitors?"

"Oh, there were beautiful women over there all right. Today they all crowded into that little closet with me, hovering around and blowing in my ear so I could hardly pay attention to my work. In fact, we just had a big party right there in the biology lab. We hired a band, and before it was all over it was the biggest party the campus had ever seen. It will be the big story on the TV news tonight."

Marni groaned appreciatively at his preposterous report, and then said softly, "I used to really get on your back, didn't I?"

"Yeah."

"I still am." With that she moved quickly behind Alex and, throwing her arms around his neck, jumped onto his back. They both laughed as Alex, whinnying like a horse, chugged breathlessly in a small circle in the living room. Times, indeed, were good!

6 | But God Can!

JEFF'S VOICE WAS LOUD as he talked to his pastor. "I'm frustrated! The more I try to find out what the Bible teaches about jealousy the more confused I get!"

He picked up his concordance and Bible that had been stacked on the desk. Gripping them so tightly that Rev. Lewis half expected to see words squeezed out the edges of the pages, Jeff said, "If you can't unravel this thing for me, I may as well give up the whole bag."

"Jeff," the pastor said confidently, "I'm sure we can clear this up. You've found pieces of the puzzle. I may add a few more. Together we'll make sense of them, and quickly."

"I hope so. 'Cause somehow it doesn't seem fair that God can be jealous, but I can't, which is what the Bible says. Look at this." Jeff shoved a pad of long yellow paper across the desk. The first page was filled with Bible references. "God is jealous all the time, Rev. Lewis."

"You've done a lot of homework, Jeff."

"I'll tell you what I did. I went through the concordance. There were forty-nine references to jealousy. Thirty-eight of them, as nearly as I can understand, have to do with God being jealous. There is one in Proverbs to the effect that jealousy arouses a husband's fury. There is one in which Paul says he is "jealous for you with a godly jealousy." Then the word is used nine times in the Book of Numbers to deal with what the husband does when he is jealous. In fact, the husband has some rights to be jealous whether he has reason to be or not; I thought that was interesting. All the other thirty-eight places talk about God being jealous. So it seems to me, from the Bible, that it must be all right to be jealous. So, what's all the fuss about?"

"What fuss?"

"Oh, uh, well, my wife, Ginger, has been a little upset lately. She says I'm jealous and that I'm not treating her right. But we're getting that worked out, so that's not important anymore. What's important is that I want to do what is right."

"I'm in favor of that," Rev. Lewis replied, smiling. "Let's sort some things out."

"Yeah."

"I'm really impressed with the effort you've put into this, Jeff. It must be pretty important to you."

"Yeah."

"One of the important things for us to understand right now is what this word meant to the writers of these passages as they described God's jealousy. The word *jealousy* is closely related to the word *zealous*. Zealous means taking care of something. Jealousy is the emotion that results when there is an infringement on one's right of possession. In most of those verses in the Old Testament, God is being protective of His right to the exclusive worship by and service of His people.

"And God has that right. His relationship to us is different from our relationship with others. He is our creator. He has known us from the beginning of time. He created us so we could worship and serve Him. This makes His rights to us and our responsibilities to Him different from those in any other relationship.

"Another way we are vastly different from God is that God's behavior is always perfect; it's an expression of His perfect wisdom and perfect love. So there is safety in letting God exercise His rights over us. If you let God control your life, that's good for you; but if you let me control your life, it won't be good because I am far from perfect.

"We are not God. We are becoming more like Him, but we will never be God. Therefore our relationship with other people will be different, especially in its limitations, from our relationship with God."

Jeff nodded that he understood, and Rev. Lewis continued.

"There are stories in the Bible that describe the consequences of jealousy even though they don't use the word. Perhaps you haven't run across those in the study you've been doing. In Genesis 37 there is the story of Joseph and his jealous older brothers. Jacob, their father, loved Joseph more than he loved his other sons, so the brothers, as you remember, sold Joseph as a slave. Jealousy came up in Joseph's life later when he was a servant to the Egyptian military officer, Potiphar. This man's wife lusted after Joseph, but he refused to go to bed with her. She was so angry she lied to her husband and told him Joseph wanted *her* to go to bed with *him*. In his jealousy Potiphar had Joseph thrown into prison.

"There was also the conflict between Saul and David. Saul's downfall began when he was jealous that the crowds were praising David more than they were praising him and he feared that the crowds would depose him. This story is a fascinating case study showing how jealousy and bitterness can consume and destroy a person. I think you would enjoy reading that, beginning at 1 Samuel 18. The stories about both these men illustrate vividly that jealousy can be deadly.

"In your study of this topic," Rev. Lewis continued, "did you look up related words such as *envy* and *covetousness?*"

"No, I was concentrating on jealousy."

"When doing a topical study it's important to include related terms and to look for principles that are conveyed through illustration as well as those that are given by clear-cut exposition. I encourage you to extend the study you are doing to include these other things."

"I see what you mean; I think I'll do that. But still, what you describe God doing—protecting what belongs to Him—is the same as I've been doing at home. I haven't given Ginger anything to complain about, really."

"If you'd like to, please tell me some more about what is happening at home. You might want to tell me some of the things Ginger is saying."

"What brought it up was that she asked to go away to a church retreat with some other couples, but I have to work that weekend. She wants to go anyway. 'No way,' I told her. Then she went into her crying thing, which proved to me that there was some reason why that retreat was so important to her. I started quizzing her about it, but she wouldn't do anything but cry."

"Which makes things pretty unpleasant for both of you."

"That's an understatement! She thinks I'm picking on her because I won't let her go, but I can't help it because I think there's more to it than she's telling me."

"Something about it makes you uneasy."

"It sure does; I can't imagine anybody getting all that upset just because they can't go someplace at great expense just to hear some guy preach all day Saturday!"

"You interpret from her attitude that there must be some other motive to explain why she wants to go?"

Jeff frowned, obviously thinking carefully, and rubbed the corner of the concordance with his thumb. "I jumped to a conclusion pretty fast, didn't I?"

"Is that what you think?"

"I'm sure of it." He stared intently at his thumbnail, a difficult question just inside his lips. Rev. Lewis saw him start to speak three times, but waited until Jeff finally asked the question that had been on his mind for several months. "What makes me so scared I'm going to lose Ginger?"

The pastor didn't have a quick answer, but he was wise, ready to help Jeff find the answer. They talked at length that day about the root causes of jealousy, and through a series of weekly sessions, some that Ginger was asked to attend, the root causes were located. Several things in Jeff's past were healed as well as recent problems in the marriage.

Ginger, by the way, attended the retreat. She came back with some new insights. Brought to awareness in God's perfect timing, she realized how she had retaliated against Jeff's panicky, heavy-handed demands.

And they lived happily ever after? No. They had something better than happiness; they had contentment in knowing they each had a spouse who could be trusted to do what was best for both of them.

Envy

7 | A Gardener's Guide to Envy

ENVY ROTS THE BONES. We learn that by reading Proverbs 14:30, if we haven't already learned it from personal experience. Envy is ugly; it's wrong; it's destructive. Envy is sand in the gears of the mind, a boil on the lips of relationship. It is an arrow that turns in midflight and pierces the heart of the envious person. We must despise it.

Because God loves us, He forbids our doing things that are destructive to us, which is one of the reasons envy is wrong (Galatians 5:19—21; 1 Peter 2:1). Envy is part of the old life, in contrast to the loving new life He promises if we trust Him (1 Corinthians 13:4—7; Titus 3:3). Envy has done as much to break relationships as any sin. We should have a healthy fear of it.

Envy is covetousness with anger. Covetousness, you recall, is longing for another's possessions. Envy goes beyond this to include resentment toward the owner of the desired object.

SEED

Envy sprouts from the belief that "I can't be happy unless I have what I want." Although this is an impractical belief, it is one of the most prevalent in our society.

61

SOIL

The misconception that personal worth is related to achievement or personal possessions is the internal condition that makes it easy for the seeds of envy to sprout. We are not valuable because of what we have or what we can do but because of who we are—valuable beings created by a sovereign heavenly Father. Our relationship with God through Christ is what matters. We need to understand that it is "whose we are" that gives us worth.

Even when we know whose we are, however, it is easy to fall into the habit of comparing our achievements or possessions with those of others. This leads us to fear that we are unable to measure up to others. Friends and family members may also make comparisons between us and others and expect more from us than we've achieved. In addition, most of us are surrounded by people who have more than we do, and when we compare ourselves with them we are likely to develop feelings of inferiority. These fearful comparisons nurture the tender sprouts of envy.

SURROUNDINGS

Our culture, including our evangelical Christian subculture, is one of the external conditions that nurtures envy because it tends to equate personal worth with achievement or possessions. Television and other media are a part of our culture that is particularly responsible for raising our expectations. Envy increases rapidly when expectations increase faster than they can be met, when demand is greater than supply. Television, far more than any other single force, raises our expectations to unrealistic levels.

Unbalanced Christian teaching also nurtures envy by glorifying those who have been materially successful and creating guilt for lack of faith among those undergoing hardship. Christ does not call us to a life of materialism. In contrast, He teaches simplicity (Matthew 6:28–34) and other-centeredness (Matthew 5:38–48). And Scripture exhorts us to keep money in proper perspective (1 Timothy 6:3–10) and to be generous in our service to others (Matthew 25:31–46; Hebrews 13:1–3). Some popular teaching in recent years has lacked this balance and has created a righteousness caste system through its implication that faith and financial success are directly related.

SUN AND WATER

Even though the conditions are right for the seed of envy to sprout, as with jealousy, we don't have to nurture it by providing the climate that allows it to come to life.

Immature Christianity is an important factor in the development of envy. Many people have the mistaken impression that Christianity is a way to get what they want. Those who have been deceived by this belief are in danger of being enveloped by the vines of envy, because Christianity provides what we need and what is best for us, but not necessarily what we want. Christianity is not a mail-order business, and the Bible is not a showroom catalog from which we can pick and choose the things that are most appealing.

Accepting the world's standards is another way we nurture envy. Advertising and examples of materialism and hedonism, even within the Christian community, will continue to bombard us. We must understand the basic principles of Christianity and do our best to resist worldly thinking patterns.

We also nurture envy by allowing prideful thoughts to tempt us. Pride is not a virtue, of course, but when it stimulates qualities we admire (industriousness, creativity, and perseverance) we often fail to identify it as the motivating factor. Consequently, we also fail to deal with it appropriately. Pride will continue to press itself upon us, and we must continue to push it back.

THORNS

The person who allows envy to flourish reaps pain. The thorns of envy are just as deadly as the thorns of jealousy.

Mental/Emotional. The envious person is riddled with painful emotions. A resentful bitterness, evident in such remarks as "It isn't fair," "I'm as good as he is," and "I deserve it, too," is prominent. The envious person makes frequent comparisons. An inactive church organist, for example, made the following comment about the person who replaced her: "She never even took lessons, and I've taught!" The envious person can never be happy because someone else always has more.

Envy makes us blind to the genuinely good things we have. Aspects of life get out of proportion. "Life ain't nothin' if you ain't got wheels," a young man once told me. This attitude causes the envious person to neglect or lose interest in what he does have. The young man who believed life was meaningful only in direct proportion to the value of his car was caught up in comparing himself with one of his friends. "Why should I put any money in this old rust bucket?" he reasoned. "I'm going to get me a new car that will make him hate his. I won't spend a dime on this one." When the car collapsed because of his neglect, the financial strain was devastating. In addition to having to pay huge repair costs, he lost a week's pay because he had no way to get to work.

Envy drops on us like rain. We shed some of it, but if we don't protect ourselves against it, it eventually soaks us, weighs us down, and pulls us into a whirlpool of self-destructive thinking and action in which we are likely to drown.

Physical. Envy causes all the physical problems associated with resentment as well as the same stress-related problems jealousy causes. Those who believe they cannot be happy without the object they desire, will not be happy. This unhappiness and discontent makes them vulnerable to depression and the symptoms often associated with it: loss of appetite and insomnia, for example.

Relational. Another response to envy, in contrast to carelessness and neglect, is possessiveness. Instead of becoming careless with possessions, the envious person may become overly possessive of what he or she has. "If I can't have what I want, I won't help anyone else get what they want," the envious person selfishly reasons. This, of course, causes alienation and may lead to retaliatory behavior when the envious person finds a target for his or her frustration.

Envy also generates rebelliousness. A man who felt alienated from his wife because she envied the circumstances of others asked a difficult question. "Why should I treat her right? I can't give her the house she wants, so she's going to put me down anyway." Envy stifles relationships.

Spiritual. Envy interferes with our relationship with God because it expresses dissatisfaction with His provisions. It's also wrong because of its destructive effects. Psalm 73 gives a vivid description of the effects of anger, but we can rejoice in the good news of verses 23 and 24.

Envy, perhaps more than any other sin, is a devastating waste of time and energy. No attitude is more empty of any kind of satisfaction than envy.

CHOPPING IT BACK

The following techniques for coping with envy will help keep the problem from becoming worse, but remember that they are just the first step toward solving the problem; they alone are not the solution.

Get to know the person you envy. Would you trade places? We are not as likely to envy a person if we know his or her circumstances. The grass on the other side of the fence only *looks* greener. And the grass on our side looks greener to everyone but us.

I recall being part of an audience of four thousand people listening to a prominent person speak. I noted his clear thinking, his smooth flow of words, and his ability to capture the attention of such a large group. As I looked around and saw people captivated by him I was impressed. No, I was not impressed—I was envious.

A week later his wife called and asked if I would see him for counseling. She described symptoms of major depression. She said he had been in tears while driving to the meeting the previous week. "I can't do it. I'll mess up. I'm not good enough to do it right," he kept repeating. Driving home, again in tears, his comments were similar: "I didn't do it well enough. I messed up. I made so many mistakes." Although extraordinarily successful, he was a man with only a marginal level of self-worth. Would I like to have his gifts? Yes! Would I trade places with him? No!

Think of the cost associated with the desired object. During the first fall that we lived in Colorado I was smitten with an overwhelming desire to have a small four-wheel-drive pickup truck. I hadn't wanted a "toy" as much as I wanted that truck since childhood. After a few weeks, all I saw on the streets were four-wheel-drive pickup trucks. "Everyone in Colorado has one but me," I said to my wife, Rachel. During a period of three or four weeks, the desire was so strong that if I saw a particularly nice truck, I would feel resentment toward the driver. That's envy, you know, and it was very uncomfortable.

However, envy began to subside when I learned the price of the truck and the cost for insurance and personal property tax. Now I have an ancient Jeep that will take me to the same places, but the total cost was not much more than taxes and insurance would have been on a new truck. Even better, with the old Jeep I can have fun bumping into rocks without fear of bruising the paint!

Envy has a way of magnifying the benefits and hiding the costs. Be sure to dig out the facts.

Avoid putting yourself in a position of weakness. While I was going through my "minitruck crisis" I didn't let myself visit a truck dealership; I was afraid I might buy a truck. That would have taken care of the envy problem, of course, but it would have added new problems. Envy had me in a weakened condition, so I guarded my behavior to avoid creating new problems.

Associate the desired item with something you value. Suppose, for example, you envy your friend's giant-screen television set. What would you give up to have it? How many days would you be willing to spend alone in your bedroom in exchange? How many bones would you be willing to have broken in exchange? How many days would you allow a loved one to go without food in exchange?

How easy to lose perspective! How easy to be ungrateful for our blessings when we give space to envy.

DIGGING OUT THE ROOTS

Envy can be transitory and short-lived or it can be an ongoing influence that perpetuates a bogus lifestyle. If our belief that worth and happiness depend on achievement or possessions is deeply entrenched, envy is likely to be an ongoing influence in our lives. Since our culture continually bombards us with this thought, it is almost inevitable that we will fall into the envy trap from time to time. The tools necessary to get at the roots of this problem are the same ones used to dig out jealousy.

Honesty. Name the problem. Don't minimize it; don't romanticize it. Envy is often associated with the color green. That is too charitable. Envy is black paint poured on the banquet table of life; it poisons and discolors everything that was set before us to enjoy.

Confession and repentance. Being ashamed of envy is proper, but it's not enough. Shame merely recognizes the immaturity of the problem; it does nothing to change it. Neither does remorse. Repentance, on the other hand, includes the intention to overcome the problem.

Self-understanding. Understand that your significance comes from who you are—God's child—not from what you have or do. The pivotal element in dealing with envy is in knowing that our value comes from whose we are. Few people realize this early in life; usually it is the culmination of a process of gradual growth and development. This is the heart of resolving the problems of envy, and it is often a long process. Ask God to develop in you the kind of perspective on the value of property that is described in Hebrews 10:34.

Problem clarification. Understanding the origin of envy is important. Where does your sense of worth come from? What are your beliefs about the pathways to happiness and contentment? How often do you compare yourself with others? What are your fears and what are you doing to overcome them?

Talking these things over with a well-informed and

trusted friend can be very helpful. This may not need to be a professionally trained counselor, but if envy is intense or if you have an underlying sense of insecurity, it would be sensible to consider professional counseling.

KEEPING FREE

These are the maintenance items. But because envy is so entwined with our maturity, the items in this section could just as easily be described as part of the healing process.

Develop a strong devotional life. Learn the joy of life in Christ. Rejoice in the particular set of gifts and circumstances God has brought to you. Rest in the assurance that it is possible to be content where you are and with what you have, as Paul learned (Philippians 4:11). This is not to say you should not set high goals. But work toward them in confidence, knowing that as you collaborate with God He will unfold things in His perfect timing.

Strive for generosity and patience. The rest will follow. Read Matthew 6:25–34 for assurance that your needs will be met if you seek first God's kingdom and His righteousness.

Tithe. Give generously of your money and time. This is one of the best ways to develop a better perspective of life.

Nurture Christian values. Allow thoughts that hurt. For example, are you willing to learn about, think about, and do something about child starvation in Haiti? About the famine in Ethiopia? About child abuse in the United States? About those in your neighborhood who are starving for friendship? Compared with your envy, how important are these issues?

In summary, envy is the least practical of all vices. There is not a shred of gratification in it. We aim it at others, but we hit ourselves. It is a distortion of healthy, wholesome ambition. Ambition gone awry becomes corrosive, contaminating the envious person and rendering that person incapable of enjoying any part of life.

8 | Anthony's Pot of Gold Without a Rainbow

ANTHONY BASCUM WAS GLAD TO ARRIVE at his apartment building and leave the car for the doorman to park. He paced restlessly in the elevator as it sped to the 32nd-floor penthouse.

Karla Moselle, his long-time roommate, rushed toward him as soon as he entered. "I was afraid you had forgotten that the Sampsons are dining with us tonight."

Anthony winced at the reminder. He had forgotten. He could think of no good reason for enduring the ponderous reminiscences of the stodgy financier nor the cotton-candy prattle of his wife, Emerald. But he knew what he and Troy Sampson had in common: greed. *I won't need him much longer,* Anthony thought. *Another major acquisition or two and Troy Sampson, whom I used to think sat on an empire, will be small potatoes by comparison.*

"Isn't anyone else coming?" Anthony asked, seeing the table set for only four.

"No. The Buckleys went to Bermuda on the spur of the moment."

When the Sampsons arrived Anthony switched into his public-relations mode. He gushed over Emerald's outfit, all but shrieked with excitement at a miniature camera Troy brought, and lavished fictitious and undeserved adulation on Troy as "the greatest innovator in finance since the inventor of folding money." His performance had the authenticity of Jack the Ripper portraying St. Francis of Assisi.

Yet Anthony showed glimpses of his true personality without realizing it. It leaked out in his condescension and in his urgent and relentless effort to be seen as being on top. He lampooned the hotel the Buckleys were staying at. He disparaged higher education. He dismissed his competitors as "the blind leading the blind."

"I had a Cadillac briefly, but I traded up as soon as I could," he bragged. He paraded the Sampsons from balcony to balcony until they never wanted to see city lights again. In sum, it was an exercise in self-aggrandizement unlikely to be equaled in this decade.

When the Sampsons left, Anthony listened expectantly for some reassurance from Karla that the evening had been successful. But she was silent while they prepared for bed. As Anthony stretched out on his back, vibrator humming quietly in the spongy depths of his mattress, he felt small, smaller, smallest. His mind took him to street level, and he looked upward. The gleaming white façade of the tall building became a massive pedestal, but there was no figure at the top.

He not only felt small; he felt empty and fragile. He felt as though he had no more substance than a discarded candy wrapper, crumpled and brittle, being swept toward the gutter. And he smelled window screen.

When he got up the next morning he was not sure if he had slept during the night or not. He decided he hadn't. He hurried to the office without breakfast, but gulped coffee and a danish during a tax-law briefing. The rest of his morning included a consultation with attorneys about a securities offering; a heated argument with a member of the board of directors whose nephew had been fired as marketing director of an obscure affiliate; a palaver with an embassy official representing a small nation where Bascum Universal hoped to extract monazite; a rapid-fire brainstorming session about corporate image; and scrutiny of a flow chart projecting installation of a new management computer.

Lunchtime. Food was brought down from the gourmet restaurant, The Top of the First, high above them. "It's just one of my little hobby businesses," Anthony enjoyed saying. "Think what it could be if I put my mind to it." They ate in the conference room while negotiating final budget adjustments. Caesar salad, martini, banter. Prime rib, baked potato, martini, discussion. Dessert, martini, heated debate. Coffee, martini, conflict. At one forty-five Anthony whispered to his secretary to bring him an Alka Seltzer. At two o'clock, on the verge of recessing the meeting because he could not control the bickering, he crumpled in pain.

He awoke the next day in intensive care. Part of him wanted to shout, "Get these tubes off me! Bring me my clothes! Get me out of here!" But part of him, the part that prevailed, was too frightened to speak.

Karla sat beside his bed, her features frozen like a cameo. She leaned forward, smiling slightly, her eyes jittery. "You're going to be all right."

Anthony had to concentrate to free his tongue, to moisten his dry lips, to form a question he didn't want to ask. "What is it?"

"It's going to be okay. Whatever it is, it's too complicated for me to explain, but they promised me it's going to be okay. You're just going to have to take it easy."

Anthony frowned, closed his eyes, frowned more deeply. He opened his eyes and stared at the ceiling, closed his eyes.

Ten days later he was out of intensive care, in a private room. Dr. Magnuson had explained the origin of the problem, the treatment plan, and a recommended lifestyle. Anthony didn't like the sound of any of it. He arranged a procession of "second" opinions, even though he trusted Dr. Magnuson as thoroughly as he ever trusted anyone. He even liked him a little— enough to listen to him when he offered some personal views about life.

"Christian, you say, Dr. Magnuson? Since I've been a man I've always thought Christianity was for the weak. Or for the meek. And I haven't seen any meek inherit the earth."

"It's brought me the only happiness I've had in my life, Anthony."

"You don't get anywhere in business without being a cynic, Doc. And I'm good at business. I calculate that half the time the goody-goody business is a cover for weakness and the other half it's a con."

"Which half am I in?"

"I haven't decided."

"Maybe you figure I'm in the weak half, and you're afraid I'll crumple if you tell me that."

"No."

"Then I'm a con?"

Anthony laughed. "Yeah! Listen to you chase me around the chess board now!" Then Anthony's face straightened and he looked intently into Magnuson's eyes. "Straight serious now, Doc."

"Yes?"

"You're trying to sell me. You want me to agree." He closed his eyes, thinking. He looked back into the doctor's eyes, "If I pay you for something it's a sale. If I pay you for nothing, it's a con. In this transaction I can't figure out if there's anything of value or not, though at times it seems that there would be. But I can't figure out what's in it for you."

"Satisfaction. I don't want to just keep you alive, I want you to live. If that happens, I've been paid."

Magnuson rose from his chair and gently squeezed Anthony's arm. "See you tomorrow." Anthony did a lot of thinking that day.

Magnuson insisted on complete care. During Anthony's convalescence he successfully barricaded him from involvement with the business. And he managed to slip a psychiatrist into the treatment program despite Anthony's cynical protests. The psychiatrist, working patiently, was able to elicit enough information from Anthony to demonstrate to him that an understanding of his personality patterns would be useful to him. And there was, much to the psychiatrist's surprise, a session in which Anthony tearfully described memories from his childhood. He relived the many nights that he sat in his bed, nose pressed against the old window screen, looking down the street hoping to see his father walking home instead of staggering home, looking at the lights of houses on the hill, promising himself that one day even more would be his. He had kept that promise beyond his wildest imagination.

But he was empty. The psychiatrist knew it by interpreting the psychological patterns; Dr. Magnuson knew it from his theology; Karla had read it a hundred times in the longing on Anthony's little-boy face; and Anthony knew it best of all, but he repeated his mistake: He again resolved to fill the inner emptiness with power and possessions. His first attempt had been futile; the second was fatal.

The psychiatrist skillfully reasoned with Anthony; Karla lovingly pleaded; Dr. Magnuson, through intercessory prayer and aided by the Holy Spirit, saw Anthony come to the point of being "almost persuaded." But Anthony Bascum remained convinced that life would be meaningless if he were not able to flaunt his superiority over everyone he met. And to Anthony superiority required power and money.

As soon as Dr. Magnuson signaled that it was all right for him to spend a few hours a day at the office Anthony entered the corporate arena with the feral abandonment of a rodeo horse. Within three weeks he was dead.

9 | Hank Hates Being a Winner

HENRY LANDSBERG WAS EVERYTHING a university dean could ask for in a young faculty member: bright, energetic, a team player, interested in research and writing. A witty lecturer, he was popular with the students. When he had arrived at this small university six years earlier, he had brought with him twelve years of heavy-duty experience in sales management with a multinational corporation and an Ivy League Ph.D. He was casual, known to everyone as Hank, but he commanded considerable respect.

Hank was everything most of his colleagues were not—he was also the perfect target of envy.

Benjamin R. Bonner was another full-time teacher in marketing. Four years younger than Hank and hired the year after Hank, Bonner was an alumnus of the university with a doctorate from a second-string university in the same state. Ben didn't have Hank's talent, but he was just as ambitious. He preferred consulting to research and spent a lot of time doing sales training and consumer surveys for area businesses.

The combination of Hank's keen academic work and Ben's enthusiastic, though sometimes imprecise, projects in the field created considerable good will among business leaders in the region. Both Hank and

Ben enjoyed their work and were optimistic about their careers.

But Ben had a problem: he was silently consumed by envy of Hank. Hank didn't know it. He assigned Ben's caustic remarks to boorishness, not recognizing they were the overflow of deep hostility. And Hank had a problem he didn't know about: unconsciously he was arrogant and condescending in his attitudes and behavior toward Ben.

Popular as he was with students, Hank felt distant from other faculty members. They rarely commented on his publications, showed little interest in collaborating on projects, and occasionally made remarks, under the guise of humor, about his workaholism. An older faculty member once chided him about his long hours by saying, "One of the things I discovered early in my career is that it pays the same whether I work myself to death or not."

Hank shrugged off the indifference—he got plenty of affirmation from students. If his colleagues were content with their level of performance, it wasn't his concern. But Ben never quit thinking about Hank's performance.

The hostile undercurrents of Ben's envy were apparent in his day-to-day comments. When Hank was named Teacher of the Year by the Student Association, Ben referred to him as Mr. Popularity for a few weeks. After the *Harvard Business Review* published Hank's article, Ben called him "our esteemed colleague, Dr. Landsberg." More routinely he resorted to preadolescent wordplays such as "Landmine" or "Iceberg" or referred to Hank's popular Introduction to Marketing course as Hanky-Panky 101.

Word came to Hank about things Ben said in his classes: "*These* are things you *can't* learn from books. If you want to know what's going on in business you have to *be there*, which is why *I'm* out there in the real world all the time. Research has a purpose, of course: it keeps the egghead professors off the streets."

Hank realized how his life was intertwined with Ben's envy when the committee on tenure made its recommendation. Tenure could be granted after six years, and usually was. But Hank was not given tenure after his sixth year. "With shrinking enrollment the legislature isn't giving the Board of Regents the freedom we used to have," the Dean explained. "It's belt-tightening time everywhere; this is going on all over." Hank accepted the bad news stoically and kept himself busy. But the next year when the tenure list was distributed, Ben, after six years, had been given tenure and Hank, after seven years, had not.

By the time Hank got home that evening he had passed through the initial stages of shock and disbelief into outrage. "Gwen," he shouted to his wife, "there's not an ounce of justice in it! It's not fair! I've done more to help the department, to help the students, to set a standard of excellence in the last seven years than Ben could do in a lifetime of trying, if he would even try. And we both know, even he knows— and it's one of the few things he might know—that he doesn't try to help the department. He's only out for himself! His getting tenure is a case in point. He's gotten next to some fat cat on the Board of Regents who has sent the word down for the chancellor to smile on him. It's an injustice, and I'm incensed over it. I'm livid!"

Gwen didn't need to be told he was livid. She understood the truth in what Hank was saying, but didn't know what to do. She wanted to reassure him. "Hank, whatever happens, whatever other people think, you and I know how well you do. We know you're a winner, that . . ."

Hank interrupted. "If being ignored, rejected, and ripped off is all it gets me, I *hate* being a winner!"

Gwen ached at Hank's disappointment. They sat, discouraged. "What can we do about it, Hank? Can we talk about it? Think about it? Pray about it?"

Hank heaved a slow, raspy sigh that sounded discouraged and cynical, but reluctance and disappointment overshadowed his cynicism. "The first thing I tried to do was pray. I don't know if I prayed or not. I feel like I've been betrayed—like God is ignoring me and that maybe He never was paying any attention to me."

"Do you mean that?" Gwen asked with astonishment and concern.

"I don't know. I don't have any idea. It just seems that this shouldn't happen two years in a row. I got out of sales management and into teaching for ethical reasons. I didn't like the tactics and the pressures my bosses put on me to push my sales force to make deals at any cost. I couldn't do that. I believed that business done by the Golden Rule could be profitable, and I thought maybe I could instill that belief into some students. It cost all of us a mountain of sacrifice and effort for me to get my Ph.D., and compared with what I was making, we give up a bundle of money every time I get paid. I thought God would notice that and protect me from getting stabbed in the back."

At that point it dawned on Hank that his reasoning was wrong. He realized he had been approaching God on the basis of his good works, believing that they would vaccinate him against the pain and discomfort of diseases that those less ethical could spread. He and Gwen discussed those thoughts, and that brought some hope; but sadness snuggled up close to Hank in bed that night.

The next morning Cliff Barnes, a graduate student who worked part-time for Ben, dropped into Hank's office. He spoke hesitantly at first, then quickly. "The word's drifting around about the tenure decisions.

Quite a few of us realize it isn't fair, and we have information that some people in administration ought to know. For one thing, when Dr. Bonner went to the regional marketing association meetings last month, he wasn't by himself. He roomed with one of the students. She says he threatened her with loss of scholarship if she didn't. He also has a way of doubling up on his expense accounts. He gets a plane ticket *and* a university car. If it's a half-day trip he drives and cashes in the ticket. Or he'll fly, and the girl will drive to wherever he's going and meet him there. I don't like it, but frankly I've got too much at stake to say anything about it. I hope someone else will." And with that he left.

Hank was surprised at himself—not by the stirrings of vengeance he felt within, but that he had not been aware of such things sooner. He was distracted all day by thoughts and plots of how he might leak the information where it would create problems for Ben.

The glee he felt when he imagined Ben being censured for his actions and perhaps facing criminal prosecution made Hank uncomfortable. Becoming aware of the sinful attitudes within him was a painful experience.

That evening Hank prayerfully and thoughtfully made a chart of Ben's actions, his own urges, and the possibilities for Christlike responses. Here is Hank's list:

Ben's Action	My Sinful Urge	Righteous Alternative
The silent treatment to me.	Avoid Ben; give him the silent treatment in return.	Maintain a civil social style; perhaps (due to the likelihood that Ben feels inferior) keep it somewhat "busi-

Ben's Action	My Sinful Urge	Righteous Alternative
		nesslike" rather than "buddy-buddy"; be congenial and open so Ben will feel accepted and free to trust me.
Malicious talk about me to others; sarcasm directly to me, sometimes in front of others.	Retaliate; show him who has the sharper, swifter verbal sword.	Confront Ben directly; use an assertive, loving style; be careful not to condemn Ben as a person, but explain how his behavior affects me.
Possible misuse of university monies, sexual harassment, and improprieties.	Write an anonymous letter to the vice-chancellor of Business; give just enough information to start an investigation; talk to the Dean of the School of Business.	Report to Ben what I have heard (but protect the source, perhaps get Cliff's permission first); ask Ben to decide for himself what he should do about these actions if indeed they are true; prepare beforehand with a lot of prayer because this will be explosive.
Possible sarcasm and childish remarks in the future.	Return the same.	Remain silent or give an honest, charitable reply when possible.

Based on Ben's actions, Hank evaluated Ben's condition and realized that despite many favorable circumstances, he was probably unhappy and empty.

Hank's sinful urge was to gloat and wish Ben misery and eternal damnation, but he couldn't forget what he knew were the righteous alternatives: to pray for Ben; to share, perhaps only silently, in his hurt; to support Ben's goals and ambitions that were worthy of support; to care for the man even though it would be impossible to support many of his actions.

As Hank studied the list for several hours he was convicted of the sinful desires within him and believed he had at least an inkling of sin's repugnance to God. His understanding was extended in both directions: He realized the evil within him was far more ugly and extensive than he had known; therefore he could no longer look at Ben with condemnation and bitterness nor respond in retaliation and hardness. But at the same time he found support in Scripture. Hope exploded within him as he glimpsed and experienced God's forgiveness, saw the possibility of God working through him, and believed God's promises. As he read from Hebrews that evening he became as joyous as he had been livid the night before. He prayed to accept the challenge: "Let us throw off everything that hinders and the sin that so easily entangles, and let us run with perseverance the race marked out for us" (12:1). Hank knew that as long as he rebelled against the actions arising from Ben's envy that he would be as handicapped as Ben. He resolved to fix his eyes on Jesus (12:2), to endure hardship as discipline (12:7), and to make every effort to live in peace (12:14). He could do this, he knew, because of God's faithfulness.

Hank was thrilled as he read, "Never will I leave you; never will I forsake you. . . . The Lord is my helper; I will not be afraid. What can man do to me?" (13:5–6). The new attitude and the work of the Holy Spirit changed Hank. He knew the change was for real when, in a faculty meeting, Ben pointed to an article about Hank in the campus newspaper and accused him of "Hanking his own horn." The group gave the pun the groan it deserved, but Hank laughed—in celebration of his walk with God that put the events of this world into proper perspective.

Lust

10 | A Gardener's Guide to Lust

LUST IS RELENTLESS PURSUIT OF ANY OBJECT. The object may be tangible (such as wealth) or intangible (such as influence). The pursuit may take place in mind only or in both mind and action. Lust is akin to idolatry and greed; in addition to being sinful, it is a reckless and impractical way to live.

We narrow our focus in this book to sexual lust, the insistent urge toward sexual possession of another person. This is a widespread problem among Christians and has not been given the attention it needs.

What's wrong with lust? It begins, after all, with legitimate and God-given feelings of sexual attraction. God has directed, however, that sexual attraction be fulfilled within marriage. Lust defies this command; its mental images strongly urge us to act upon them (Matthew 5:27–30).

More common among Christians than actual immoral behavior, I think, is for lust to lead to a fantasy world that becomes more powerful and more compelling than reality. Lustful fantasy makes reality drab and uneventful by comparison. Living in a fantasy world deprives us of joyful partnership with God, and the opportunity to experience His life-changing work is lost. Lust causes preoccupation with self; which breeds confusion and leads away from life.

Lust is damaging to a marriage because the partner is less perfect than the fantasy. Minor faults or defects are magnified by comparison. The lust-prone spouse is easily angered and is dissatisfied because neither self nor others can sustain in reality the standard portrayed in the fantasies.

If the fantasies of a lustful person are known, they may provoke fear in the person who is the object of lust or lead that person into sinful behavior. Lust is also likely to provoke jealousy in a third party who has an emotional claim on the lusted-after person.

Lust can move from a level at which it is manageable—when it can be "turned on or off"—to an obsession, which is a pathological condition that is very disruptive. You will read in chapter 12 how destructive that can be.

Almost everyone fantasizes about sex. Of the 106,000 respondents to the extensive survey on sexual attitudes and behavior conducted by *Cosmopolitan* in 1980,[1] 97.5 percent reported having fantasies about sexual involvement. When fantasies are of sexual involvement that does not contradict God's law about sexual activity, they should not be labeled lust and are not wrong. But 68 percent of the *Cosmo Report* respondents reported sexual fantasies involving people they knew but to whom they were not married. These data are similar to that presented on men in an earlier major study.[2] Such fantasies are wrong.

I doubt that the data would be much different for Christians. Lust is a wonderfully private sin. Clinical experience has convinced me that lust is a problem of extraordinary prevalence among serious Christians.

[1] Linda Wolfe, *The Cosmo Report* (New York: Bantam Books, 1982).
[2] A. C. Kinsey, W. B. Pomeroy, and C. E. Martin, *Sexual Behavior in the Human Male* (Philadelphia: W. B. Saunders Company, 1948).

The Cosmo Report says that because sexual fantasies are so common, we should not feel guilty about them. Wrong! This is drawing a conclusion from creature habits rather than from our creator's likeness. Majority rule is not our standard; God's word is. I'm not as interested in how many people fail to conform to God's standard as I am in learning to conform to it myself. I would like to help you, too, if I can; that's the purpose of this book.

SEED

There is one crucial element that gives life to the problem of lust: the belief that "sex is love," "sex is power," or "sex is necessary." When this belief is coupled with the willingness to substitute fantasy relationships for real relationships, lust is almost inevitable.

SOIL

Unrealized expectations are one of the internal conditions that make it easy for the seeds of lust to sprout. We expect relationships to be perfect. The sudden realization that they're not may lead to lust, a solo activity, because it seems safer. Unsatisfactory relationships may be caused by the failure to learn social practices that lead to good relationships. Those who are overly demanding, possessive, or fearful are likely to have disappointing relationships. Unfortunately, the person who pursues lustful fantasies often has not experienced real love or known truth and trust in any personal encounter. Consequently, he or she mistakenly concludes that a perfect fantasy is preferable to an imperfect personal relationship.

The emotional effect of stifled relationships is another internal condition that causes lust to sprout. Sometimes healthy relationships, not necessarily sexual, with the opposite sex are stifled at a critical stage. If appropriate behavior is thwarted in early adolescence when sexual changes are taking place and there is strong sexual curiosity, fantasizing may result. The availability of prurient movies and pornographic materials makes this especially likely.

The mistaken notion that sexual arousal or activity validates one's identity also encourages lust to sprout. This factor is more significant when the problem is actual physical involvement with another person than when the problem is limited to lustful thinking. Some persons actually believe they are more alive and more worthwhile when they are sexually aroused. They have failed to find the multitude of other superior means of involvement with life, and they have failed to comprehend and receive identity and worth by virtue of being God's creation.

SURROUNDINGS

The external factors that contribute to the development of lust are many and varied. Some are more powerful than others, but we need to keep our guard up against all of them.

The absence of valuable, mutually enjoyable, mature friendships. As mentioned previously, the person most vulnerable to lustful thinking or behavior is one who fears relational failure. But anyone, even those of us who are blessed with an abundance of mature friendships, are more vulnerable to lustful thinking when those outlets are not available to us. This could be the case, for example, during an extended business trip.

Friends who condone lust, initiate it, or encourage it. Shoptalk in nearly every occupation is likely to be peppered with sexual jokes, sexual observations about others, and innuendos about sexual activity.

Media bombardment of distorted beliefs about sex and its importance. Advertising tantalizes us visually as well as through seductive music and tone of voice.

An unsatisfying marriage. When a marriage is not emotionally gratifying, the temptation to look outside marriage is strong. Furthermore, an emotionally ungratifying marriage cannot possibly be as physically gratifying as it might be, which only compounds and complicates the problem.

The opportunities to indulge in lust are too numerous to mention. Behavior and topics of conversation are often deliberately tantalizing. Commercial enterprises based on lust—printed pornography, peep shows, sexual phone calls, and so on—have grown to tremendous proportions. A recent newspaper article reported that a company that sells the services of men and women to participate in obscene phone conversations (approximately one dollar per minute; use your charge card) was depositing eight million dollars per month in its bank account. Lust, like all the other sins, is big business.

SUN AND WATER

What conditions do we control that help lust grow? Our major contribution is sloppy thinking. Here are some common rationalizations we use to justify lustful thinking or action. Do you recognize yourself in any of these?

"Lust is a substitute for an affair." Perhaps. But it's still wrong, because it defies God's law and because it ultimately destroys relationships with others.

"I do it by myself; it doesn't hurt anyone else." Wrong. When it hurts you, it hurts those whom you could better serve and be an example to. Preoccupation with and time spent in lustful activities can lead to an

isolated and even fearful mental outlook on life. When you spend money on lustful behavior or paraphernalia, you support a decadent industry that degrades all humankind.

"Christ has forgiven all my sins: past, present, and future." True. Praise the Lord! But have you invited Him to be just your Savior or to be Lord of your life as well?

"Sex is a need, therefore whatever it takes to fulfill the need is okay." Partly true, partly false. It is true that the Bible describes sexual activity within marriage as a need, instructing married couples to fulfill their partner's sexual needs (1 Corinthians 7:2–5). And the Bible points out that sexual impulse is strong and may be difficult to control (Matthew 5:32). But this does not justify improper fulfillment. The healthy sexual desires of a married person can be satisfied within marriage. If they are not, the couple should work on the problem rather than substitute a different, and worse, problem.

Healthy sexual desires of unmarried persons can be brought to a manageable level by developing other desires that are equally attractive, equally enjoyable, and equally meaningful when fulfilled. I am personally acquainted with many celibate persons who are divorced, widowed, or medically unable to be sexually active within a marriage who report that life is just as meaningful and complete without sex as it was with sex. These people have thriving interests in areas such as travel, music, teaching, or athletics. They feel whole and, they tell me, joyously fulfilled—without sex.

It pleases God to be asked to help us with such conditions. He never leaves us in a position in which sin is our only option. *Never!*

"I deserve a little entertainment." Probably so. But lust is sin, not entertainment.

"Everybody does it." Probably not. But so what? Are you following everybody or following God?

"I can't help it." Wrong! You can help it. You may not have tried, however. Perhaps you have nurtured lustful thinking into a deeply ingrained habit. If so, it will be difficult to help it, *but help it you can.* And since it always pleases God to help us fight sin, you will have His all-powerful assistance.

"Pornography is an outlet that diminishes sexual crime." It is not and does not. The viewing of pornography *increases* sexual crime.

Dr. Victor B. Cline, of the University of Utah, has conducted a comprehensive study of the effects of pornography as reported in scientific journals. He states that the destructive effects of pornography have been clearly established by "a flood of well-done behavioral studies by researchers that . . . have repeatedly given documentation of potential harm to consumers of aggressive erotic materials—especially males."[3]

The connection between pornography and sexual crime was obscured by a report by the federal government's Commission on Obscenity and Pornography,[4] which reported failure to find a causal relationship between crime and the pursuit of pornographic activities. This report was sharply criticized from the outset,[5] and many respected researchers are convinced there is a relationship. Dr. Cline says that the evidence is really quite overwhelming on this issue.

[3]Report from Second National Consultation on Obesity, Pornography, and Indecency, 15. (Consultation held September 6-7, 1984, Cincinnati, Ohio.) Report is available from Citizens Concerned for Community Values, c/o College Hill Presbyterian Church, 5742 Hamilton Avenue, Cincinnati, Ohio 45224.

[4]*The Report of the Commission on Obscenity and Pornography* (Washington, D.C.: U.S. Government Printing Office, 1970).

[5]See "Pornography Revisited: Where to Draw the Line," *Time,* April 5, 1971; critique by Victor B. Cline, Ph.D., *Psychiatric News,* June 7, 1972.

Dr. Harold Voth, a senior psychiatrist at the famed Menninger Foundation, states that pornography is "harmful, sick and destructive." He continues by saying that pornography "suggests behavior to people who would never have thought of it in the first place. I have seen cases where it made people behave less civilized. It emphasizes the perversions." Dr. P. Susan Penfold, associate professor of psychiatry at the University of British Columbia, says that pornography "provides the rationale for rape, child sexual abuse, and the battering of women. Pornography makes the act of rape seem to be energetic or better-quality intercourse. It makes wife-beating seem to be superior foreplay, and child abuse as a needed initiation into sex." Based on records of the Michigan State Police, a study of 38,000 reported sexual assault cases in Michigan during the years 1956 through 1979 determined that in forty-one percent of those cases pornography was used just prior to or during the sex crime.

Even if it were true that pornography diminished the frequency of sexual crime, allowing pornography would still not be the best way to deal with the problem. Crime diminishes only when persons, individually and collectively, live by God's patterns.

All of this should be irrelevant to the Christian who, I hope, would not be content to merely avoid major crime but would instead seek the best possible relationships with God and others. Operating contrary to God's law is always costly. The genuine believer would not be willing to carry the limitations imposed by the thorns of lust. God desires abundant living for each of us, but His plan for an abundant life does not include lust.

THORNS

Lust, like every other sin, has damaging effects. Putting them in the same categories we used for jealousy and envy, they are as follows:

Mental/Emotional. Those who are aware of their guilt in regard to lustful behavior are fortunate. That awareness and the accompanying sense of shame are devices God uses to warn of the even greater problems that casual lust leads to. When lust begins, the lusting person can usually "switch it on or off." But as more time is given to it, it becomes more and more important, and thought control becomes more and more difficult. I remember a comment by one man whose lustful thoughts had become an obsession. "I haven't had any enjoyment from my lustful thoughts for fifteen years," he said. "The thoughts I have, the scenes I have in my mind, are disgusting to me—they nauseate me—but I can't stop them."

When a person begins to seek out pornographic magazines or movies or to participate in other lustful activities, the habit becomes very expensive, in both time and money. In addition, shame and fear of being found out usually increase at this stage. And there is often a fear similar to that of persons with other addictions—that the supply of gratification will disappear.

Physical. Again, there are likely to be stress-related complications.

Relational. Lust often leads to a self-consciousness, especially when it involves furtively seeking out pornography shops, peep shows, bars with nude dancers, or such places. The self-consciousness is often a barrier to relationships, especially for the person who (quite properly) feels a sense of guilt.

Unrealistic expectations about the physical appearance or sexual behavior of another person are another source of relational problems. Many men and women have entered marriage with unattainable expectations for the partner due to earlier involvement in salacious fantasy.

Pornography in any form degrades not only those

individuals depicted, but all those they represent—all women, all men, all children. It frays the bonds of mutual respect that are necessary to hold society together.

Spiritual. Lust is wrong, God says. What else can it do, then, but build a barrier between us and God? Prudent Christians will follow the advice of Romans 13:14: "Clothe yourselves with the Lord Jesus Christ, and do not think about how to gratify the desires of the sinful nature." Disobedience leads to God's wrath (Ephesians 5:6) whereas those who "get rid of all moral filth and the evil that is so prevalent and humbly accept the word planted in you . . . will be blessed" (James 1:21, 25). It is in God's plan to bless those who live in His fellowship. This is a lifestyle quite different from self-centered indulgence. Self-acceptance and genuine caring for others is in His plan for you.

CHOPPING IT BACK

The starting point of change is deciding you want to be different. This in itself is likely to be an agonizing struggle, but becoming vividly aware of the cost of lust is the best place to begin. Consider what damage the thorns of lust are doing in your life, and determine the cost of repairing it. Is it worth it? Until you decide it is not, you are not likely to change. The serious Christian, however, will ask God to reveal the costs. This step requires courage because God most certainly will show that the costs of disobedience are indeed high.

Here are some strategies to help you cope with lustful thinking. You may find one or two of them particularly helpful, but you will need to use them vigorously for quite some time to combat your habits. It is necessary, however, to work toward ultimate resolution and healing of the underlying causes.

Pray. You'll need to pray specifically and often. Ask

God to give you the purity of thinking that is characteristic of Christ.

Replace destructive thoughts. Lust is a sin of the mind, first of all, so it is important to displace destructive lustful thoughts with thoughts that are neutral or constructive. The section entitled "Stopping Unwanted Thoughts" in chapter 14 suggests specific ways to do this.

Avoid temptation. In other words, "Cross the street." Several alcoholics have told me they have changed grocery stores, learned new routes to work, or stopped going to restaurants that serve alcohol to minimize exposure to temptation. Breaking the pattern of lust requires similar strategies. It may mean avoiding certain places or people. Whatever it is, do it.

Face reality. Take the magic out of your fantasies. You aren't going to have an affair with the playmate of the month. Dream dreams, yes! But dream dreams that are good for you, dreams that God can help you achieve.

Consider the consequences. Look down the road. Anticipate your regrets. It's true that one phase of sin leads to another. Do you really want to gather the thorny harvest that lustful thinking produces?

Consider the victims. Who are you helping to degrade by your lustful behavior, and who in the lust industry are you supporting? Do you want to support an industry that exploits women and children in pornography films? That promotes sadomasochistic sexual behavior? That lauds bestiality?

Would you recommend your behavior to your son or daughter? To your parents, to other Christians, to persons you admire? Would a friend carry out the behavior you imagine? Would you be surprised to see someone you know in a pornographic movie or magazine? Is using it any less sinful than participating in or producing it? Ask yourself if the child you once were would be proud of the person you are?

Consider the time. The time you spend in lust competes with the time and emotional energy you have available for God and others? Who will not know God because you have destroyed your effectiveness by pursuing your passions instead of your commitment to God?

Visualize your behavior. Imagine having your thoughts and actions brought to life on a movie screen in front of all the people you admire and work with.

DIGGING OUT THE ROOTS

The roots of lust grow like those of dandelions: straight down and deep. And the longer they're left unattended, the deeper they grow and the more difficult it is to dig them out. If part of the root is left in the ground, however, a new plant will grow. The tools needed to dig out the roots of lust are the same as those used for jealousy and envy.

Honesty. Name the problem. If you have gotten yourself intertwined in the vines of lust, they won't release you without a struggle, and they won't be less damaging if you call them something else. The sooner you quit rationalizing, the sooner you can free yourself.

Confession and repentance. Shame is not repentance; repentance includes the intention to quit. Because lust is mental and therefore so convenient to engage in, you can expect failure along the way. Authentic repentance recognizes that lapses of performance are inevitable, but carries a strong intention to avoid them.

Self-understanding. Healthy relationships are necessary for a healthy self-concept. All of us need a good relationship with God, with at least one male friend, and with at least one female friend. We also need either a healthy relationship with our parents or the healing of those relationships if they are unsatisfactory.

We all need outlets for worshiping God, friends who affirm and help us, activities we enjoy and find meaningful, and to love and be loved. We also need an ongoing "quota" of reassurance, hugs, counsel, and admiration. Seek fulfillment of these. All are available to the person who seeks God's pattern in developing relationships. Those who substitute fantasy for reality may do so because of a lack of relational skills. They may lack assertiveness, be overdependent, or be bound by fear. Or perhaps their relational skills have grown weak for lack of use. Whatever the case, these skills are necessary and can best be developed with the assistance of another person.

It's essential that we fulfill our needs for relationships with relationships that are real, not with cheap imitations such as fantasies and other lustful behavior.

Problem clarification. Study the origins of the problem (Seed, Soil, Surroundings, Sun and Water) described earlier in this chapter. Talk through these issues with a well-informed and caring person whom you can trust to give you an honest judgment and to maintain confidentiality. Determine what is or has been missing from your life that you have tried to compensate for with lust-related thoughts and actions. If you conclude that inadequate or unhealthy relationships have contributed to your problem, it is important that these relationships be healed. This may require that you forgive someone who has hurt you. Before peace can be realized, memories of past pain and sinful behavior must be acknowledged and healed.

Get the help you need to understand the problem.

An impasse in growth may occur if you do not reach out for help. Thinking is not distorted by honesty, so the help of a trusted friend or counselor who can maintain mental honesty and determination is valuable.

KEEPING FREE

Temptations to lust will continue to bombard us, and lust will continue to sprout. We must therefore exercise some maintenance methods to keep the weed from growing.

Develop a strong devotional life. The joy of life in Christ is one of the most effective deterrents to sinful habits. (This is the third time those two sentences have been used in this book. How important do *you* think this concept is?)

Choose your geography wisely. This is the "cross the street" coping technique. This may mean that you avoid driving down the street on which the porn shop or peep show is located; it may mean that you hop out of bed more quickly in the morning instead of staying there to fantasize and masturbate; it may mean extraordinary discretion in choosing movies or reading material; it may mean staying away from locations where the problem is the greatest. Find other places to go and things to do that are constructive and wholesome.

Identify vulnerable times. Temptation is particularly difficult to resist following occasions of unusual stress or rejection. And many women can identify a pattern of sexual urge synchronous with their menstrual cycles. Recognizing patterns and cycles of vulnerability will help us anticipate days when we need to be particularly alert to sexual temptation.[6]

[6]K. Dalton, *Once a Month* (Pomona: Hunter House, 1979).

Pursue your needs sensibly. Work carefully and decisively toward fulfilling your needs. Even though progress may seem slow, proceed in a steady and sensible way. Don't settle for what is available just because it's easily achievable; pursue what you actually need.

Guard your thoughts. Our thought life is important to God. In Matthew 15:19 Jesus lists evil thoughts alongside sins we generally consider far more serious: murder, adultery, sexual immorality, theft, false testimony, slander. So put healthy ingredients into your mind. Consider Paul's advice: "If you believe in goodness and if you value the approval of God, fix your minds on whatever is true and honorable and just and pure and lovely and praiseworthy. Model your conduct on what you have learned from me, on what I have told you and shown you, and you will find that the God of peace will be with you" (Philippians 4:8–9 PHILLIPS). That is another way of phrasing the computer-industry maxim "Garbage in, garbage out." In Christ's words, "Set your heart on his kingdom and his goodness, and all these things will come to you as a matter of course" (Matthew 6:33 PHILLIPS).

Pursue a lifestyle based on truth. As you begin practicing Christlike behavior, you will find other persons treating you with more respect and appreciation. Reality will become more interesting and active; it will be a more than adequate substitute for fantasy.

The following two chapters show how these principles worked in the lives of two people. Bonnie Bascum had an "ordinary" level of lust. Mike's problem was more serious; lust had become pathological for him. As you compare the two, however, do not be misled into thinking that Bonnie's less complicated condition was any less repugnant to God than Mike's extensive and sordid story.

11 | Bonnie Takes a Lesson to School

THROUGHOUT THE SUMMER Bonnie found herself escaping into fantasy whenever minor irritations arose. It was a wonderful change from the pressures of parenting and the disappointment of feeling like a single parent with a husband in the house.

Her fantasies were generally romantic but not sexual. Sometimes the leading man was Toby Forrester; other times he would look like Don but have Toby's warm and affirming style. Sometimes the man was not a person but a presence of strength, security, and, above all, interest in her.

At first the fantasies had no plot; they were brief vignettes in which she and Toby were together—in his office discussing a school project for which he was praising her for her leadership; in her living room, looking at carpet and fabric swatches as he praised her good taste; or enjoying a lavish candlelight dinner in a nearby city after having addressed a convention as chosen representatives of the school board.

As weeks went by, however, the fantasies became longer, developed threads of a plot, and began including more explicit sexual behavior. As the fantasies grew, so did Bonnie's uneasiness. This increased the distance between Bonnie and Don, but Don did not notice. Bonnie's attempts to get Don more involved in the marriage were somewhat timid because she felt guilty about her fantasies. She didn't ask him with enough assertiveness to get his attention, but she felt rejected by his failure to respond nonetheless and would retreat into another fantasy. The cycle kept itself going.

During the early part of the summer most of Bonnie's fantasies were during natural breaks in her household work or late at night when she couldn't go to sleep promptly. As the summer progressed they became more frequent. She would lapse into a fantasy while working or she would lie down on the couch to enjoy one as a reward for hard work. And she more frequently began one when she went to bed. She was getting hooked.

She had not seen Toby Forrester all summer. She looked forward to fall when her responsibilities as a room mother would take her to school. But she had some apprehensions. She wondered, half hoping and half afraid, if some of her fantasies would come true. She worried that she might make a fool of herself in front of Toby, and she worried about the status of her marriage.

She did not like having secrets from Don. Occasionally he would speak to her while she was lost in her fantasy, and she would not realize it. Don commented once about her daydreaming, and that had frightened her enough to "swear off" indulging in fantasy for nearly a week.

The week before school, Bonnie attended a meeting for new room mothers and saw Toby for the first time in three months. She had half hoped that he would have turned ugly, tasteless, and repugnant during the summer. Not at all! When he spoke to her she felt a definite sexual stirring. During the next two months her fantasies were deliberately sexual. The first time she thought about Toby while making love with Don she felt ashamed and promised herself she wouldn't do it again. But she did.

Although things between Don and her seemed better, she was alarmed because she knew it was only because she had been substituting Toby's face for Don's when they were together.

Near suppertime one November day Don started to make a telephone call. He held up a note pad lying beside the phone. "What the crud is this?" He laughed. "Look at this doodling, Bon. Didra must have a boyfriend!"

Ornate inch-high initials in the center of the pad were edged by a lacy scallop and a border of tiny hearts. There were other hearts scattered about the page with the same initials, T.F., in them.

"Who's T.F.?"

Bonnie, almost gasping in panic, croaked, "How would I know? There's hundreds of kids her age." She felt as if she were trying to balance on a swaying telephone wire high above the ground.

"I'll kid her a little when she comes down for supper," Don said.

"Don't do that," Bonnie said hastily. "Kids her age are sensitive about things like that. Let me have the pad."

Don held it behind his back. "I won't hurt her."

Didra found the paper sticking out from under her plate. "What's this?"

Her father replied, "I don't know. Maybe you can tell us."

"I never saw it before," Didra said. "Who's T.F.?"

Don looked at Chad who glanced at the paper and said decisively, "Don't ask me."

Don was puzzled. He thought Didra must be lying, but he knew that was unlike her. He looked at Bonnie in confusion. "We'll talk about it after supper," she said quickly.

It seemed like a last meal on death row to Bonnie. She couldn't decide whether to tell the truth or not. She was in deep now. She could have lied out of it earlier by telling Don the initials were her girlfriend's or by contriving a story about a neighbor coming in to use the phone or something—anything—but how could she tell him the truth without blowing their marriage to dust?

As the family ate in silence, she could see Don's mood shift from confusion to gloom to anger. After supper Don shooed the kids to their rooms and motioned Bonnie to sit back down at the table. Don sat directly across from her, arms folded, forearms against the table and his hands gripping his elbows. His voice was husky and breathy. "It's yours, isn't it! You've got a boyfriend. You're having an affair, aren't you!"

The words accused, but the voice pleaded for disproof.

"I'm not, Don. I swear I'm not."

"If you're not, what's some guy's initials doing in hearts? What do you call that if it's not having an affair?"

"I call it misery! I call it being the biggest fool in the world! There really isn't any man—there isn't anybody to have an affair with—there isn't . . ."

"Don't play games with me! There's initials, there must be a man. Who's T.F.?"

"Let me explain. It's all silliness. It's terrible, but it's silliness. I feel awful. I've felt terrible all fall. But I haven't done anything. I swear I haven't done anything."

"You're writing a guy's initials all over a paper like a crazy eighth grader! What else have you done?"

Bonnie sighed. "Let me get my breath back. I want to tell you everything. You've got to let me tell you. It's not as bad as you think. This man, he doesn't even know I've been thinking about him. And that's all I've been doing—thinking. It hasn't been right; I know that. But that's all I've done—just think. And I haven't even wanted to, not lately at least. I got caught up in it, and I didn't know how to stop, and I didn't know how to get any help to stop. Just let me talk about it. I want to get over it." She rested her arms and head on the table and cried.

Don's head whirred with questions he wanted to ask, reassurances he wanted to extract. It took them several hours to say all that had been stored up during the many years they had neglected their marriage. Bonnie discovered that Don had felt pushed aside as she devoted herself to the children and community service. Don discovered how important it was to Bonnie to be reassured of her significance. He also learned how meaningful to her his seemingly small kindnesses and compliments could be. They concluded the discussion with a deeper understanding of one another, confidence about the future of their marriage, and a decision to seek pastoral counseling.

During counseling Bonnie first learned to reconstruct her habit patterns. She followed the approach described in chapter 14. She learned about the internal conditions that had to be corrected so that lust would not easily sprout. She grew in her sense of self-worth.

The marriage became more meaningful to both of them as they kept communication up to date. Don said, "After what we've talked about so far, I guess we can talk about anything in the future." They saw to it that they did.

Don helped her work her way out of the problem. He attended parent's meetings at school. This relieved his suspicions about Toby Forrester and helped Bonnie disrupt her fantasy patterns by providing some "interference" in her images.

Physical attractiveness is closely correlated with

emotional significance. As Don began listening better, taking more interest in Bonnie, and as they began sharing more activities, he became more and more attractive to her. The "real thing" far excelled the best fantasy.

The pastoral counselor helped them understand God's principles for marriage. As they followed them, their marriage became the focal point of life, and the fringe activities became even better than they had been.

By the end of the school year Bonnie had broken the habit and was free of shame. Don recognized Bonnie's needs and interests and was responsive to them. They were finally free to talk about everything that was important to them.

"The lesson I've learned," Bonnie said one day with a sparkle in her eye, "is that a principle can be more valuable than a principal." And there wasn't a doubt in Don's mind about what she meant.

12 | Lust Was Mike's Hobby Until ...

MIKE WAS YELLING. "I'm already late for work, so leave me alone, Beth, will ya? Just leave me alone! I swear, if I was a dog, you'd hafta be a flea!"

"I just want to know—are you going to see the marriage counselor with me next week or not?"

"I'll go! I'll go! But only if you'll listen to him when he tells you to get off my back. You're driving me out of my mind. A wife is supposed to be helpful. You remind me of that line in *Funny Girl*, 'I wanted a lift and you kicked me!'"

Beth saw Mike's scowl, heard the raw edge in his voice, and assumed it was anger; she did not recognize it as the intense fear that it was.

Mike stomped to the car and drove wildly to the shop, punched in on time, and hurried to his machine without talking to anyone. He wanted his mind hypnotized by the rhythmic bash! whirrr! chong! of the machine as it shaped, drilled, and trimmed. He knew the machine would produce 47,850 parts for a computer without him this shift if all went well. Meantime, what would he think about?

He didn't want to think about Beth. She was miserable, and he felt responsible. But he felt powerless to help her and angry at himself for being powerless to control his own behavior for so long, let alone help her. He was part of her problem, but who would help him with his? Not Beth; she didn't even know about his problems. *If she only knew,* he thought, but it all seemed hopeless, and he wondered again if suicide was the only way out.

Beth, meantime, got ready for her first appointment with Dr. Lake, a Christian counselor. She was apprehensive but hopeful that at last the marriage could begin to improve. She decided almost at once to trust Dr. Lake. After some background information about herself, she told him why she had come.

"I found a dirty magazine under the seat of Mike's car. It was a terrible thing, and I didn't know what to do. I hoped it belonged to somebody else. I finally showed it to Mike, and he just laughed and pulled another one from under some socks in his dresser drawer.

" 'All men look at these,' Mike said to me, 'and I'm a man.'

"So I screamed at him and told him, 'Real men don't have to tell themselves they're real men!'

"That set things off in a hurry! We went 'round and 'round with another argument, and that was that. We haven't been happy for several years. The marriage fell apart a long time ago, I guess, and maybe it can't be repaired—ever."

She trembled at the thought, realizing that she was frightened, frustrated, and angry. She continued rapidly.

"With this new situation, I don't know what to do. Should I get a divorce? Sex therapy? Some provocative negligee? I got a catalog from a place called Naughty Nighties. Should I get some of those things so I'll be more appealing in the bedroom? What's the matter with me, and what do I do about it?"

She started to rush breathlessly on to more questions, but Dr. Lake motioned for her to pause.

"Let me answer those questions first, and then we'll move on to more," he said with warmth and authority. "Divorce? No. Let's concentrate on finding out what the basic, underlying problems are, first. We don't have those answers yet. Sex therapy? I doubt it, because when a couple has had happy sexual adjustment in the past, as you told me the two of you had until a few years ago, adjustment nearly always returns when the emotional problems are resolved. A nightie? It won't resolve the basic problem, but if it would help the two of you enjoy being together, that would be wonderful. It would be a pleasant supplement, but in itself, not enough."

Beth continued with urgency in her voice. "My girlfriend said to make him jealous. She said that snapped her husband out of it."

Dr. Lake replied slowly, "Mike's drowning, so turn the fire hose on him?"

"Then let him learn how to swim!"

"He's drowning, so throw him a book?"

"But Dr. Lake," Beth pleaded, "look what he's doing to me."

"Yes, and that's significant. But wouldn't you agree that we should *also* find out what this is doing to *him?* And what's *causing* what he's doing? Porn is wrong; I don't condone it. Usually, however, interest in pornography is a symptom of a more basic problem or combination of problems. I hope Mike will talk with me about it and let me know him well enough—including the deeper, hidden parts of his life—so we can work together to find out the origin of the difficulties in his life and in your marriage. Will he come in?"

"I think so. He sort of said he would."

"Good! We'll start with that, then."

A week from that evening Mike was in Dr. Lake's office enthusiastically describing Beth's faults. "I try to make a good life for her but she frustrates my every move! If I painted the ceiling of the Sistine Chapel, she'd paste wallpaper over it. Nag, nag, nag, Doc! So, can I help it if other women look good to me?"

"I don't know if you can control that or not, Mike. What *can* you control in your life?"

Mike stopped. He knew the ugly truth—that he no longer controlled his lustful thinking. He knew the sordid chain of sexual perversions he had participated in during the last four years. He knew the futility, the emptiness, the illusion and deceit, and the moral/ mental/spiritual cancer of his behavior, and he hated the cold-sweat trembling terror he experienced each time he realized he could not control his thinking. Lustful thoughts bombarded his mind—he saw the images of nude women superimposed on the machinery at the shop; he imagined intercourse with every woman he saw; his concentration on any task was interrupted every few seconds by lustful daydreams. And with it, always shame and fear.

He had to decide whether or not to talk about it with Dr. Lake. He weighed the pain of telling against the pain of carrying the burden alone and decided to trust the counselor.

"What can I control? Almost nothing. I'm just barely hanging on." With carefully chosen words, his eyes toward the floor, Mike quietly described the sequence of involvement from lustful imagination to the many other activities that had brought him to the point of despair.

"And now my mind just keeps on doing what I've taught it to do: think sex. The only time it changes subjects is when I hate myself. Like this morning. I woke up with the sensation that I'd been grabbed by the legs and was being whirled around and around. It seemed like my blood had rushed to my head and the pressure was building and building till I thought my skull would split. Sometimes I wish it would; then it would all be over. But I don't think that very often.

"Most of the time I just have a dull disgust—a real foul, dirty attitude toward myself. Not hating myself; it's worse than that. I used to hate myself, so I know what that's like. It's bad when you hate yourself, but at least there's energy.

"With this other thing I don't even care to do anything with myself—for or against. I just look at myself and want to turn away. I think, 'Phew! don't even look at yourself—you're too ugly.'

"Now *that's* dying—when you're so turned off to being you that you don't even want to admit you exist. That's a lot worse than being angry with yourself, because when you're angry with yourself at least you're involved. With this condition, you wipe yourself clear out of existence and, like I said, if *that* isn't dying, what is?"

Mike leaned forward, looked Dr. Lake in the eye, and said, "I can't stand it anymore! Is there any hope?"

The counselor assured him there was but that the process would be painful, that failure would intrude itself into progress, and that adequate reconstruction could not take place without God's involvement.

"If that's what it takes, I'll consider it," Mike replied.

They met twice a week for two months, then weekly for three more. A lot happened. At the end of that time Dr. Lake wrote a summary of the case and Mike compiled some principles and observations about the development of lust. Here is what Dr. Lake wrote:

> Mike has a brother, six years older. During childhood the parents dealt with the two boys in a way that gave Mike the impression that his older brother could do no wrong and that he, Mike, could do nothing right. Both parents were very busy with careers when Mike was born, so often,

when he needed something, they gave him a cookie or a toy to placate him. In this environment Mike came to believe he was inferior and that physical gratification is the best solution to frustration.

During early adolescence Mike was shy and socially inhibited. When he was about fifteen, he discovered that lustful thinking could lead to physical gratification and that it gave him a sense of power and control. In his earliest fantasies Mike was usually a hero receiving the adulation of girls his age, much to the consternation of male peers.

During his early twenties Mike gained social skills, engaged in appropriate courtship behavior, and married Beth at age twenty-three. A strong undercurrent of self-doubt remained, however, and when Mike was nonassertive he would retreat to lustful thinking to bolster his self-esteem. He also used lustful thinking to counteract boredom, especially on the job.

When Mike and Beth's second child was born, increased financial pressures and recurring comparisons with his older brother (by now a successful realtor) began to discourage Mike. He began buying pornographic magazines, triggering a progression of inappropriate sexual activity: attending pornographic movies and live shows, seeking out more sordid magazines and shows, visiting massage parlors and prostitutes, and becoming sexually involved with women he met at work. This progression occurred over a period of four years and was marked with increasing sexual fantasy to the point of obsession. Concurrent with this were fear of disease, fear of getting caught, and a strong sense of guilt and shame. During the year before entering treatment, he suffered depressive symptoms and severe anxiety about losing his family and of losing control of himself.

These conditions made it very difficult for him to be comfortable with Beth. Sensing that something was wrong, she initially showed more interest in him, but because he felt unworthy, he rejected that. She felt hurt and angry and reacted with passive-aggressive retaliation.

During five months of individual counseling Mike made a commitment to Christ, confessing and repenting to God of his sins. We spent time praying for guidance, and Mike prayed twice daily for understanding and for courage to use his new understanding.

Mike realized his anger toward his parents for favoring (inadvertently, we believe) his brother and was able to forgive them. After several weeks of prayer Mike concluded that the Lord was not directing him to speak to either of his parents about it, but he discussed it with his brother, and they are finding a new and valuable friendship.

We also worked on assertiveness skills by developing a stronger sense of self-esteem (which was now possible with Mike's new understanding of his personhood as God's son) and using behavioral methods to help him change thought patterns. With greater assertiveness and growth in self-esteem both he and Beth have been more comfortable in the marriage. We will now begin a series of sessions to help them heal the wounds they have inflicted on one another and develop a strong foundation upon which the future of the marriage can be built. Mike and I rejoice in the Lord's goodness, for it is He who has brought healing to Mike!

Mike clarified many things in his mind. Here is how he explained it:

I made up some principles and have some comments about each one:

1. When you get into lust, you cannot go back to a lower level and be satisfied. It keeps pushing you toward fantasies or activities that get more and more bizarre, more and more dangerous.

2. Sin is fun at first, but the fun doesn't last. Everything I tried got old after a while—usually pretty soon. Then I'd get some new idea, always thinking I could feel as good again as I did at first. But there are two things wrong with that: First, you can only feel as good as you have recently felt, and that's nothing like how you felt at first. Second, when you get a new idea you never think of the bad consequences. I would ignore the fear and guilt and shame and self-loathing I had just been going through and pretend, "Hey! This is going to be it!" What stupidity! But, that's the nature of temptation—deceit.

3. Physical pleasure won't fix emotional hurt; neither will physical or emotional pleasure fill spiritual emptiness. I was empty emotionally and spiritually, in large part due to some mistakes my parents made, even though they were very loving. I tried to fill the emptiness with the wrong things—first with fantasy and then with more active mental-physical sensations. It didn't work for me, and it never will for anyone. I hope you don't make the same mistakes.

4. Fantasy is more perfect than the real world. This caused me to lose interest in what was real and pushed me to spend more and more time in fantasy. Eventually I couldn't tell the difference. That's when things started going wacko real fast. This stage always happens a lot sooner than you would think; it happens before you know it because the change is part of the real world and the person caught up in fantasy is living in a phony world and is uninterested in the real world. I hope you won't let it happen to you.

5. Lust in your mind is destructive. It's an invisible stain. At first you are confident that no one knows what you are thinking, but after a while you begin to wonder and you start getting suspicious and wanting to hold yourself away from people, which adds more problems. It nearly wrecked my marriage.

6. God makes all the difference in the world. The damage that comes from lustful fantasy is not so much from what the fantasy turns to but from the fact that in lust you turn away from God. There isn't anyone who is strong enough to do without God. A verse I memorized recently is Mark 12:30: "Love the Lord your God with all your heart and with all your soul and with all your mind and with all your strength." That command doesn't leave any room for dirty thinking.

Another verse that has been helpful is Colossians 3:23: "Whatever you do, work at it with all your heart, as working for the Lord, not for men." That reminds me that I belong to the Lord; it motivates me to control my thoughts and actions. It brings more meaning into my work at the shop, too.

7. God does what we can't. At first I could do very little to control my own thinking, so God helped me a great deal. As I cleared up some of the confusion from my childhood and grew in maturity and strength, I was able to control more. God continued to supply what I couldn't supply, but because of my growth in Christian maturity, I can take more responsibility than I used to. I rejoice in that evidence of God's grace to me.

8. Things don't change instantly. But as soon as I realized that God was helping me and found out what it meant to be accepted by Him I had hope. That's when my life began to turn around.

9. The problem is at two levels, and both need to be taken care of. In my case, the problem at the

deep level was my feeling of unworthiness, which led to fear in many social situations. So I would escape into fantasy. When fantasy lost its appeal I got involved with more active sexual sins. This began creating new problems: I lost control over my fantasies and our marriage went downhill. I'm convinced that it would not have been possible to improve the second level of problems without first taking care of the deeper problem. That could not have happened without God's help!

10. We face temptation forever. I still have to fight it, but I have a lot of victory over the temptation to lust. Now I find that there are some temptations that I hadn't been aware of before. God and I will face those together, though, and through His grace we'll be victorious! Resisting temptation is an opportunity to grow in maturity. It's important to me to keep up Bible study and prayer so that when I'm in the middle of resisting temptation, I can approach God freely and boldly and ask for His help.

Dr. Lake had occasional sessions with Mike and Beth together during these months to encourage them to have hope, to support one another, and to grow in spiritual commitment to the marriage. They found that praying together on behalf of the marriage helped them understand each other and to take initiative in apologizing for their own sins against the other.

Then they began a series of sessions to help them increase relational skills and to make sure they had forgiven one another for the wounds of the past. They realized this was not the end of their problems, because problems will exist as long as Satan is alive in the world. But, they were creating a three-partner marriage: God, Mike, and Beth. They rejoiced in that and looked forward with eagerness to the future.

Oh, yes. Every once in a while they got a package— a very small package—from Naughty Nighties.

13 | "But Your Boss Is a Man!"

IN EIGHT YEARS OF MARRIAGE Lisa and Harry had never had a conflict like this one. They stood facing each other across the corner of the bed. Harry was yelling.

"No way on earth will I let you go away four days with your boss, Lisa! When you took the job you said it wouldn't interfere with us. Now look what you're up to!"

"Listen to what you're saying, Harry Grayfield. You're accusing me of something that hasn't happened and never will! I've never even thought of that, and you've condemned me already. Why don't you heat up a branding iron and burn an 'A' on my forehead right now. That seems to be what you want—just to push me into the ground."

"No, I don't. But four days in Houston in the same hotel? No trade show keeps people so busy they can't get into trouble! I know what can happen; I can see the handwriting on the wall. People are . . . "

"You've been reading too much handwriting on *bathroom* walls," Lisa broke in. "*That's* where your mind is. What makes you take such juicy pleasure in accusing me? Do *you* have something to hide?"

She stomped out of the room as Harry stood open-mouthed, feeling incredibly tiny and weak. When she slammed the door their wedding picture jarred off the wall and dropped out of sight behind the dresser.

The problem stalled at that point for three days. They knew they needed to talk about it and come to a resolution they could both accept, but neither wanted to talk first.

At supper one evening Harry, patting his pudding nervously with his spoon, said, "Well, I guess we better talk some more about your problem."

Lisa clenched her teeth at the words "your problem" but had already promised herself that she would carry her part of the conversation with maturity.

"We do need to talk about it, Harry, and I'm glad you want to. It's something that we need to work out together. We both know I need to work and that the job I have as a service representative for such a prestigious company would be hard to replace. And even if I changed jobs it would probably mean trading problems, not being free from problems."

"Yeah," Harry replied, "if it's not one thing it's another. So what do we do with this thing?"

"Well, first of all, Harry, I want to make sure you understand that I love you and no one else. And it's important to me to please God through sexual faithfulness and to be as trustworthy as I can possibly be. Don't you believe that?"

"Sure, I believe that," Harry said. He reached over and clasped her arm. "I believe you and I trust you." He squeezed her arm and they smiled at one another.

Then Harry pulled back and straightened up. "But I don't have any reason in the world to trust Adam Nash. The guy is thirty-nine years old, probably in the middle of a midlife crisis, probably runs around all the time. Who knows what kind of stunts he's going to pull? Why should I trust him?"

"You don't have to trust him; you can trust *me!*"

"Somehow that doesn't seem like enough, Lisa.

Forgive me, 'cause I know it should be enough, but I know what men are like. I see what goes on at our office. Sooner or later every man down there makes a move on someone. Some of the guys all the time, but sooner or later it's everyone. At least he would want to."

"Including you?"

"Well, uh, yeah, of course. I fight it away. But it scares me, temptation like that does. I don't like it, but it's there. So I know what goes on."

"Thanks for saying that. I don't know if men are like that any more than women are or not, especially nowadays. But it's obvious that both of us have to contend with temptation and difficult circumstances in this part of life. I guess it wouldn't be any easier for one of us than it would be for the other. What can we do about it?"

"I was wondering, Lisa, if we could write down some principles to follow, and then make a list of the things we would or would not do to make sure we follow those principles."

"Good idea," Lisa said warmly. She stood up to move toward Harry, and he rose to meet her.

"I'm sorry about . . ." they said in unison. They laughed, and the knowledge that they both were ready to apologize and forgive brought them a sense of relief and optimism. They moved to the sofa so they could sit comfortably. They talked intimately and found one another more interesting than making a list that evening.

But thinking through and listing solutions to the shared and frequent problem was important. During three conversations later in the week they wrote these guidelines for on-the-job relationships with members of the opposite sex:

Principles:
What we believe we should do
1. Avoid temptation.
2. Live as a witness of God's work so unbelievers will want to know Him.
3. Avoid the appearance of evil so others will not be led astray.
4. Respect our spouse's weaknesses. Although we recognize that neither of us can keep the other person from feeling jealous, we will avoid situations, attitudes, and talk that put pressure on the other.

Practices:
How we will follow the principles
1. Maintain a strong personal commitment to God and to living by His plan.
2. Read the Bible and pray together as regularly as possible.
3. Keep open and complete communication with each other.
4. In the natural course of conversations at work, let others know our values and the importance of those values. This can be done in ways that are not "holier than thou." While we will not condemn others, we can still describe our own moral boundaries.
5. When a working relationship is close, communication about moral boundaries should be particularly straightforward.
6. Avoid situations that are "personally social." We will attend the important social activities that are sponsored by the work group.
7. Pray regularly for co-workers.
8. Watch for opportunities to witness, as the Holy Spirit leads, to all those around us.

With these guidelines it was fairly easy for Lisa and Harry to discuss the business trip she had been assigned. Lisa knew she would be spending many hours with Adam as they staffed the display booth at the trade show. She decided she would refuse to have dinner with him, and she felt she would be more comfortable if she flew to Houston on a different flight than Adam, reasoning that this would thwart any inference Adam might make that she was interested in him. She also remembered that an old friend lived in a Houston suburb and wrote to her inquiring if they could get together. This additional accountability might be useful.

It was good that she and Harry had anticipated the issues because a couple weeks before the trip Adam began making suggestive comments: "These business trips aren't all work, you know . . . Houston's a great city; there are some places I want you to see while we're there. . . . The woman who went to the trade show with me last year got promoted, you know."

Lisa and Harry prayed together about how Lisa should reply to Adam's persistent hints. Talking and praying about it together reassured and strengthened both of them, but it was not clear to either of them whether or not Lisa should say anything specific, so they waited for direction from the Holy Spirit.

The time to be specific was obvious enough when it arrived. Adam said, "I have two rooms reserved at the hotel in Houston. Maybe we only need one?" It was a question.

"Adam," Lisa replied, "you're an attractive man in a lot of ways. But, two rooms. I'm *working* for the company, but I'm *living* for another man."

"Will he be in Houston with us?" Adam persisted.

"In a way, yes. Harry's just as important to me when I'm in Houston by myself as when we're together. Harry's number one."

"You sure?"

"Sure."

"I'm not surprised," Adam said. "You're different. I

thought so all along. You're special, and you're honest."

Lisa smiled. "I hope so." Then she got an idea and quickly added, "Maybe I'm not so honest. I just lied to you."

"What do you mean?" Adam asked hopefully.

"I said Harry's number one. Actually there are two number one's in my life."

That grabbed Adam's attention.

"There's my husband, and there's God."

Adam stared in disbelief. An unfamiliar discomposure rippled through him as he groped for words with which to regain control of the conversation. He wasn't used to this; he had no glib line. He stammered, "I don't know whether to cuss or genuflect, Lisa." He rubbed the back of his neck and added slowly, "Look, this trip, it'll be just like you want it. Just like Harry wants it, even. No hassles from me—okay?"

"Okay."

It was. Things went well at the trade show, resulting in some changes in both their job descriptions when they returned. The new assignments would require Lisa and Adam to work together more, both in the office and traveling. Lisa and Harry discussed this change, and Lisa decided she should talk explicitly with Adam, which she did.

"Adam," she began, "our duties are going to require us to spend a lot of time together, in the office and away from the office. I think we can be a strong working team."

Adam nodded in agreement.

"If tensions build up between us, it could spoil the opportunity we have to be a strong team and to benefit professionally."

Adam again nodded.

"But we could anticipate what tensions might

develop and take steps ahead of time to minimize the tension."

He wasn't sure where the conversation was going, so he was guarded. "That makes sense to me."

"Adam, the area I'm specifically thinking of is the sexual area. You've felt some attraction to me; you said so after we got back from Houston. And I know that if I let it develop I would be strongly attracted physically to you. I don't want that to happen because I have a strong commitment to my husband. He and I believe our bodies belong to each other and to no one else. That commitment is a mental decision, backed up by actions, and this is one of the actions I need to take. I ask you to respect my limit in this part of my life. Please don't nudge me toward physical involvement. Not even a little, either verbally or in what you do."

Lisa was uncomfortable but continued. "There will be a payoff for both of us from that, I believe: We'll be more at ease with each other, knowing that there won't be a personal crisis between us down the road. We can be fully relaxed and creative in our work, because we have agreed to do what will be best for both of us in the long run. What do you think?"

Adam was thoughtful for what seemed like more than the actual minute before he replied. "You're right. Absolutely right. In a way, I wish you weren't, but you are." He smiled a bit, shaking his head slowly. "I can't believe I'm glad you're right about that." He extended his hand. "You've got a deal."

Claiming
the Victory

14 | How to Deal With Temptation

PERHAPS THE ONLY PEOPLE who think they aren't tempted are the ones who yield so fast they don't notice. We are all tempted—often. John Bunyan suggested that the temptations in youth are of the flesh, in middle age of power, in later years of covetousness. The kind of temptation changes, but its relentless attack continues.

Spiritual growth does not eliminate temptation. John Wycliffe put it this way: "Let no man think himself to be holy because he is not tempted, for the holiest and highest in life have the most temptations. The higher the hill, the greater is the wind; so, the higher the life, the stronger is the temptation of the enemy." Temptation is something we will deal with throughout life.

WHAT IS TEMPTATION?

Temptation is an urge to disobey God. It is an inner appeal or enticement to do wrong, which is usually accompanied by the illusion that pleasure or gain will result.

SATAN IS THE ONLY SOURCE OF TEMPTATION

From the moment Satan tempted Eve (Genesis 3) to the time he tempted Jesus (Matthew 4:1—11) to the most recent temptation you have had—he has always been the sole supplier. God does not tempt anyone. "When tempted, no one should say, 'God is tempting me.' For God cannot be tempted by evil, nor does he tempt anyone; but each one is tempted when, by his own evil desire, he is dragged away and enticed" (James 1:13–14). "The cravings of sinful man . . . [come] not from the Father but from the world" (1 John 2:16). "The world" in this verse means Satan and his forces.

WHY DOES SATAN TEMPT US?

God and Satan are at war. Satan's hatred for our redemption and righteousness is exceeded only by God's love for us. God *will* win the war, but meanwhile, we are drawn into the conflict and choose, in each temptation, whom we will serve.

Temptation is Satan's recruitment technique—his primary weapon in his battle to control our allegiance. Satan wants to dominate us; it is against him that we struggle in life. "For our struggle is not against flesh and blood, but against the rulers, against the authorities, against the powers of this dark world and against the spiritual forces of evil in the heavenly realms" (Ephesians 6:12).

SIN IS ATTRACTIVE

Sin is turning away from God, rejecting His offer of life and fellowship, disobeying His commands. Sin is totally destructive in the long run, but it can't be all unpleasant or it wouldn't be so popular! People don't sin because they have to; they sin because they want to—it looks like fun, and for the moment, it is fun.

Consider the appeal of the fruit to Eve: good for food, pleasing to the eye, and leading to wisdom. It appealed to her physically, emotionally, mentally. It hooked her God-given desires through her senses and affections; and once acted upon, it became her master.

"The wages of sin is death" (Romans 6:23) in this life and the next. Even when we know that, sin still appeals to us. Why?

TEMPTATION IS BUILT UPON DECEIT

Satan is a deceiver. Jesus said, "When he lies, he speaks his native language, for he is a liar and the father of lies" (John 8:44). He is cunning beyond our comprehension, and he uses a multitude of tricks to trap us. He lies to us as he did to Eve (Genesis 3:4—5), he misuses Scriptures (Matthew 4:6), he tries to outwit us with subtle schemes (2 Corinthians 2:11), and can even disguise himself as a true believer (2 Corinthians 11:14). Thus temptations usually appear to make sense. "There is a way that seems right to a man, but in the end it leads to death" (Proverbs 14:12).

Satan often avoids a direct attack, but sows seeds of doubt, unbelief, and rebellion through false teachers (2 Peter 2; 1 Timothy 4:1), ungodly friends (1 Corinthians 15:33), and nurtures the evil that is within us. "For out of the heart come evil thoughts, murder, adultery, sexual immorality, theft, false testimony, slander" (Matthew 15:19).

He may appeal more openly. Proverbs describes folly as a person crying out to passersby, "Stolen water is sweet; food eaten in secret is delicious" (Proverbs 9:13—18). Whatever the approach, he is active in his pursuit. "Your enemy the devil prowls around like a roaring lion looking for someone to devour" (1 Peter 5:8).

THE RESULTS OF TEMPTATION

Temptation begins a chain of events that leads to death. "Each one is tempted when, by his own evil desire, he is dragged away and enticed. Then, after desire has conceived, it gives birth to sin; and sin, when it is full-grown, gives birth to death" (James 1:14—15). Temptation fans desire (which is inclined toward evil anyway). If desire is not controlled, it leads to sin, which always leads to death. Temptation, desire, decision, sin, death is the sequence that Satan, the enemy of our souls, wants us to follow.

TEMPTATION IS NOT SIN

Christ, who was and is sinless, was tempted (Matthew 4:1—11; Mark 1:12—13; Luke 4:1—13). He "suffered when he was tempted" (Hebrews 2:18), but He did not sin: "tempted in every way, just as we are— yet was without sin" (Hebrews 4:15).

Temptation is similar to a physical reflex—a stimulus followed by an immediate response. An elephant steps on your foot: pain! Stimulus, response. Open your lunch bucket and a bird flies out: surprise! Stimulus, response.

You find out that your neighbor has won a free trip to Europe: envy. Stimulus, response. Sin? I think not. You quit talking to that neighbor. You allow resentment to fester in your heart. You try to figure out how to take a trip that will overshadow your neighbor's. Sin? Yes, because you have had the time and opportunity to control your thinking and behavior. You entertained temptation, and *chose* your thinking and behavior.

It is sin when we seek out stimuli that incline us toward evil. It is sin when we forgo the discipline that leads to spiritual growth. God's plan is for us to grow in discipline so that we can resist the stimuli that bring out dangerous responses. It is not sin when Satan attacks us with tempting outside forces or when the nature of Satan arises from within us and entices us toward evil attitudes or actions. Temptation itself is not sin, but flirting with it, refusing to defend against it, and yielding to it are, and they separate us from the abundant life God has promised believers.

WE CAN RESIST TEMPTATION

Satan wants us to yield to temptation, so he will take us as close to the limit of our resistance as he can, but he cannot take us to the limit. God has promised that He, God, "will not let you be tempted beyond what you can bear. But when you are tempted, he [God] will also provide a way out so that you can stand up under it" (1 Corinthians 10:13).

We will choose to sin, though we don't have to. We will struggle, as Paul did (Romans 7:7–15), but we will emerge victorious! Thank you, God, for assurance of victory and change (Romans 8 and 12).

The great array of Satan's forces—awesome opposition—is lined up against us but is unable to force us to sin if we know how to resist.

HOW TO RESIST TEMPTATION

Pray for protection. "Pray that you will not fall into temptation" (Luke 22:40), Jesus recommends. As in the Lord's Prayer, pray "lead us not into temptation" (Matthew 6:13) regularly.

Don't feel guilty. Temptation is not wrong so don't condemn yourself for being tempted. Put your energy into the fight against it. Self-condemnation and doubt about who we are in Christ come from Satan.

Avoid exposure to temptation. Some persons are so allergic to bee stings that one sting could kill them. They stay away from bees! Each of us has areas of life in which we are particularly vulnerable. Know yours, and stay off the premises!

Think protectively. "Be self-controlled and alert," Peter writes. "Your enemy the devil prowls around like a roaring lion looking for someone to devour" (1 Peter 5:8). Paul cautions, "If someone is caught in a sin, you who are spiritual should restore him gently. But watch yourself, or you also may be tempted" (Galatians 6:1).

Resist quickly. Do not play with temptation. "Do not give the devil a foothold" (Ephesians 4:27).

Remember the source. Temptation is from Satan. He has one goal: your death.

Recognize temptation as a deceit. A service club I once belonged to held a trivia contest among the members. The prize, obviously not announced in advance, was a gold-painted cow chip. Temptation is a gilded cow chip; scrape the surface, see what's underneath, and it won't be so attractive.

Test your thinking. Use two questions to challenge your mind: First, is the *desire* sinful? Study James 1:13–15 carefully until you are convinced of the danger of following improper desires. Second, is the *means* through which you plan to fulfill the desire sinful?

Stifle the urge to rationalize sinful behavior with devious logic. Be alert to rationalizations in your thinking. If you find one, stomp on it! Kick shabby thinking out of your mind.

Know you are "more than a conqueror." You *can* get past temptation successfully. Read Romans 8:28–39 and 1 Corinthians 10:13.

Realize that yielding is a choice. We'd rather pretend otherwise and say later, "The devil made me do it!" but he didn't. He wanted you to; he tried to get you to; he made it look attractive. Period. He didn't *make* you do it. You did it. Don't allow thoughts that lead you astray. Throw faulty thinking down the toilet.

Think of the consequences. "The surest protection against temptation is cowardice," said Mark Twain, and he was partly correct. While we know that God's protection is more powerful than our cowardice, a healthy dose of fear can be very valuable. Think clearly about the embarrassing, painful, wounding outcome of giving in to temptation. Such thoughts are not much fun, but they are beneficial!

Pray while tempted. Use the quick crisis prayer Mike used in chapter 12. Ask God to give you the characteristics of Jesus that are opposite the problem you face. Mike, you recall, was troubled by lustful fantasy, and so he prayed for purity similar to Jesus' purity in his own mind. Here are some other examples. You'll benefit by adding some of your own to the list.

Man's problem	Jesus' characteristic
envy, hatred, indifference	love
turmoil, anxiety	peace, sound thinking
restlessness	patience
selfishness	kindness
condemning spirit	acceptance
infidelity	faithfulness
abusiveness	gentleness
procrastination, laziness	self-control
stealing	trustworthiness, sharing
lying	honesty
prejudice	understanding, love
timidity	courage, discipline
lust, immorality	purity

Remember that help is available through prayer. There is completeness in the Incarnation—Christ's living on earth in human form—for through this we know that He understands fully our experience. "Because he himself suffered when he was tempted, he is able to help those who are being tempted" (Hebrews 2:18). Ask!

Prayer gives us the power to repudiate Satan. "Submit yourselves, then, to God. Resist the devil, and he will flee from you" (James 4:7). Claim, in prayer, your inheritance as a child of God: "You have been given fullness in Christ, who is the head over every power and authority" (Colossians 2:10). Having the new nature within, we can take our stand against the devil's schemes (Ephesians 6:10–18). We can then repudiate Satan's false claims on us; we are not his, we belong to God, who has qualified us "to share in the inheritance of the saints in the kingdom of light" (Colossians 1:12). Satan has no place in this kingdom, but we do!

Therefore, we may pray boldly in the name of Jesus Christ to rebuke the forces of evil. We may, as God's children, affirm our defiance of Satan's deceitful appeals. Put on the armor and fight!

Read Scripture. These passages are reassuring during times of temptation: Psalms 3–6; 10–18; 34; 40; 71; Romans 8; 2 Peter 2:9; Hebrews 2:18; 2 Corinthians 12:9; John 17:15; 1 John 5:4; James 1:12.

Maintain healthy activities. The best defense is a good offense, many coaches say, and they have a good point. Be involved in what is wholesome. Find new activities for your time and thoughts. Invest your energies in building up relationships between yourself and others.

A. *Maintain a regular devotional life.* A consistent system for this will help: study materials, a quiet place, and a regular time.

B. *Find and get to know Christians who will encourage you and hold you accountable.* Our "brothers throughout the world are undergoing the same kind of sufferings" (1 Peter 5:9). We can draw comfort from that; we have a responsibility to others to hold firm.

C. *Participate in the things that contribute to your growth in understanding and practice of the faith,* because they will help you avoid and resist temptation: Bible study; being part of a small group in which to learn and to give and receive support; regular and active participation in corporate worship; prayer time with spouse or family; communication with the Lord at brief intervals throughout your daily routine. "Put on the full armor of God so that you can take your stand against the devil's schemes" (Ephesians 6:11; also read verses 10–18).

Anticipate the benefits from the times of testing you will experience. Temptation is a "crucible" experience through which we can become purer, stronger, and more like Jesus. Take hope in that.

Don't expect a perfect performance. If you expect your performance to be better than Paul's, read Romans 7:7–25, a passage about his struggle with sin. Strive for perfection, but rejoice in knowing that God's gracious mercy covers our failure!

STOPPING UNWANTED THOUGHTS

God has more ways of helping us stop unwanted thoughts than we could fit on a list a mile long. Here are three approaches to help combat them.

1. *The "12:21" method.* This is an application of Romans 12:21: "Do not be overcome by evil, but overcome evil with good." It has two parts.

A. *Say "STOP"* immediately when an unwanted thought intrudes. If you are alone, say it aloud. Speak with energy and authority. Mean it! If you cannot say it aloud, shout it in your mind with the same energy and authority as if you were saying it aloud.

This involves choice—you must choose to oppose the unwanted thought. And as soon as you move from thought to action, the choice is reinforced. When you say it aloud you give it greater strength because it goes through sensory channels.

B. *Crowd out the unwanted thought.* Immediately after saying "STOP," crowd out the unwanted thought with something better. This is the principle of *displacement:* pushing out the old by moving in something new, overcoming evil with good.

Initially, the new thought may be almost anything: counting, counting backward from three hundred by sevens, reciting the alphabet, reciting the alphabet backward, touching various textures within reach, or noticing how many shades of green you can see from where you are. Anything you think about that is neutral is better than the unwanted thought that is negative.

The goal, however, is to replace negative thoughts with positive ones, not just neutral ones. Far better than counting or reciting the alphabet are singing or humming a hymn, praying, reading something inspirational, reciting a Bible verse, counting your blessings, or giving yourself a compliment.

This method has helped thousands to renew their minds (Romans 12:2). There is considerable research evidence from the fields of psychology and psychiatry to document its effectiveness. Long-embedded habit patterns, naturally, require longer to change, but many find considerable improvement in two weeks. Practice must be consistent, but you *can* change your mental patterns!

2. *Memory healing.* Our memory of old actions and their consequences is often a garbage heap that provides the breeding ground for pesky unwanted thoughts. God can clean up that old mess by healing memories of old events that stimulate bad thinking.

As a counselor and friend, I have been thrilled to be present on a number of occasions when God has worked in this way. Those who are most able to receive God's help, I have observed, are those who are fully committed to Him and who are putting that commitment into action as best they can.

The healing of memories is a large, significant topic. To do it justice would require a separate book, so

I have only listed it here, not explained it. Virtually everyone carries wounds from the past that remain unhealed. The healing process frequently requires forgiveness, restitution, face-to-face reconciliation (but let the Holy Spirit guide you), and always God's direct intervention. Usually a considerable amount of time in learning, remembering, reflecting and understanding, and confession and repentance precede readiness for healing prayer. All of this is best done with trustworthy, competent counseling assistance and support. Study the books listed at the end of this chapter for a better understanding of this process.

3. *Seek God's new nature.* Our new self "is being renewed in knowledge in the image of its Creator" (Colossians 3:10; also read verses 1–17). Without a commitment to be God's person, the other strategies cannot achieve success.

God is at work in our lives. He is changing us now. When the Holy Spirit controls us, He will produce fruit in our lives: "love, joy, peace, patience, kindness, goodness, faithfulness, gentleness and self-control . . ." (Galatians 5:22–23). If we are seeking holiness, the Holy Spirit is producing it in us. It doesn't happen at once (would that it did!), but it *is* happening (Hebrews 10:14). Rejoice—aloud if you can—that this is so!

BENEFITS OF RESISTING TEMPTATION

We are called to believe in the person of the Lord Jesus Christ. True belief will be expressed in lifestyle. "Let us put aside the deeds of darkness and put on the armor of light. Let us behave decently, as in the daytime, not in orgies and drunkenness, not in sexual immorality and debauchery, not in dissension and jealousy. Rather, clothe yourselves with the Lord Jesus Christ, and do not think about how to gratify the desires of the sinful nature" (Romans 13:12–14).

This shift in lifestyle brings us into opposition with Satan. He tempts us—tries to lure us into disobedience. Temptation is an ordeal, but good can come from it. God can recycle and renew anything. Even Satan's temptations can be used by God in His process of building us up.

"Consider it pure joy, my brothers, whenever you face trials of many kinds, because you know that the testing of your faith develops perseverance" (James 1:2–3). I won't speak for you, but pure joy is pretty scarce during my trials.

Thank you, Lord, that you've always seen me through, pure joy or no. Thank you, Lord, for your promises of support; help me know them; help me change.

William Penn said "God is better served in resisting a temptation to evil than in many formal prayers." Resisting temptation must be to God a very meaningful act of worship because it is a voluntary and purposeful action. Obedience is being a doer, not a hearer only (James 1:22), a high form of worship.

The righteous "will be like a tree planted by the water that sends out its roots by the stream. It does not fear when heat comes; its leaves are always green. It has no worries in a year of drought and never fails to bear fruit" (Jeremiah 17:8). That beats jealousy, envy, and lust. You're not sure? Trust me.

Obedience pays in eternity. "He who overcomes will inherit all this [heaven], and I will be his God and he will be my son" (Revelation 21:7). You're not sure? Trust the Bible.

Obedience pays in this life. "The man who looks intently into the perfect law that gives freedom, and continues to do this, not forgetting what he has heard, but doing it—he will be blessed in what he does" (James 1:25). You're not sure? Trust Christ.

15 | Fences of Freedom

THROUGHOUT THIS BOOK are a number of dog-
matic statements. These are necessary because God
has absolute commands for us to follow, and if this
book is to be consistent with the Bible, the absolutes
must be included.

Here's another one: Obedience to God's law is
essential. Ephesians 5:6 says, "Let no one deceive you
with empty words, for because of such things God's
wrath comes on those who are disobedient." There will
come a day, we read in Matthew 25:31–33 and
Romans 2:7–8, when we will be judged. Judgment
would be unfair, indeed it would be impossible, if there
were no standards against which judgment could take
place, but God's law is the standard.

We must understand the eternal consequences of
God's law even though it can seem very harsh and
punitive. God's commands often seem like limitations
on life. It is true that they limit our behavior, but they
do not limit life; they expand it.

God's laws may seem to some like an obstacle
course—a long series of interruptions and nuisances
to avoid or overcome along the journey to heaven. Seen
in this perspective, life is difficult and unappealing—a
long struggle in which a capricious God surprises us
with new barriers and hardships. This is a mistaken

understanding of God, His dealings with us, and the purpose of His law.

LAW IS LOVE

From my office window I can see a small, three-story building with a flat roof. The rooftop is about the size of a tennis court, and I can picture how it would look if it had a tennis net stretched across the middle. There is a wall and railing around the edge of the roof, but I can imagine it without those—tennis court straight to the edge and then an abrupt drop to the sidewalk. I wouldn't want to play tennis up there, would you? Forced to, it would be a cautious game as we pinged the ball back and forth with the most timid of strokes.

On the other hand, if the rooftop were surrounded by a strong, twelve-foot-high fence, we could enjoy playing tennis there because the fence would give us security. We would have the freedom to run for the shot and to concentrate on the game without having to worry about plummeting off the edge.

God's laws are a fence. "God is love" (1 John 4:16), and His laws are expressions of that love. They give us boundaries within which we are secure; they give us freedom to "get into" the game of life.

We may lower the fence and defy the natural consequences by playing without it, but that would be foolish because we would have to play timid or plummet.

Or we could deny the importance of the fence. We could make a hole in it so we could slip back and forth from one side to the other. We might think, mistakenly, that we would have more freedom, but we wouldn't. It's always dangerous on the wrong side of the fence.

But there's another problem. When we meddle with the fence, we're not in the game. When we lower it or cut holes in it, we have our back to the game. We are no longer enjoying the game or our partner, and we forfeit the chance to benefit from our partner's expertise or to win the game.

INVINCIBLE PARTNERSHIP

God and I could beat you and your partner at tennis. Me? I'm no kind of player. But what a partner! Invincible!

We can team with God in life if we wish. Do you have the invincible partner on your side of the net? Are you giving Him space on the court, or have you foolishly crowded Him off?

God offers us His care: "For the pagans run after all these things, and your heavenly Father knows that you need them" (Matthew 6:32; see also 1 Peter 5:7; Luke 12:7; Psalm 115:12). God offers protection: "As the mountains surround Jerusalem, so the Lord surrounds his people both now and forever more" (Psalm 125:2; see also Psalm 34:7 and 91:4). He offers us His wisdom: "If any of you lacks wisdom, he should ask God, who gives generously to all without finding fault, and it will be given to him" (James 1:5; see also Ecclesiastes 2:26; Daniel 2:21; Luke 21:15).

As the angel told Mary, "Nothing is impossible with God" (Luke 1:37). We are told that "God has the power to help or to overthrow" (2 Chronicles 25:8). God did this for David: "My hand will sustain him; surely my arm will strengthen him" (Psalm 89:21). Paul found God's strength equally available: "I can do everything through him who gives me strength" (Philippians 4:13).

We, too, can work in partnership with the invincible partner. "My flesh and my heart may fail," we can say with the psalmist, "but God is the strength of my heart and my portion forever" (Psalm 73:26).

PERFECT FRIEND

God is loving. God is powerful. God is our perfect friend. He is always nearby. "The Lord is near to all who call on him, to all who call on him in truth" (Psalm 145:18; see also Psalm 16:8; 34:18; Acts 17:27). Abraham called God "friend" (James 2:23). He will never leave us nor forsake us (Deuteronomy 31:6; Hebrews 13:5).

His compassion never fails (Lamentations 3:22). He understands us perfectly (Psalm 119:168; 139:3; Proverbs 5:21; Jeremiah 32:19). And He loves us enough to change radically the quality of our lives.

"At one time we too were foolish, disobedient, deceived and enslaved by all kinds of passions and pleasures. We lived in malice and envy, being hated and hating one another. But when the kindness and love of God our Savior appeared, he saved us, not because of righteous things we had done, but because of his mercy. He saved us through the washing of rebirth and renewal by the Holy Spirit, whom he poured out on us generously through Jesus Christ our Savior, so that, having been justified by his grace, we might become heirs having the hope of eternal life" (Titus 3:3–7).

Let us take advantage of all that God offers. He is inside the fence with us, which makes it the best place to be. Staying within the fence protects us from evil without that can break us, from evil within that can rot us. Let us keep the fence strong and rejoice in the freedom that it brings. Let us thank God for the fence of His law!

"This is love for God: to obey his commands. And his commands are not burdensome, for everyone born of God overcomes the world. This is the victory that has overcome the world, even our faith. Who is it that overcomes the world? Only he who believes that Jesus is the Son of God" (1 John 5:3–5).

Get to know God. Learn to *really* live!

16 | Here's How to Really Live

KNOW GOD. KNOW WHAT HE WANTS FROM YOU and what He wants for you. Give God a chance to teach you how much He loves you.

Look at God instead of at yourself. Staring into your navel makes you cross-eyed.

Listen to God. Listening to yourself too much scrambles your mind.

Reach toward God. Grabbing for all the gusto you can get breaks your arms.

Learn to love others unselfishly. Find out how much freedom that gives you.

Get smart. A good way to begin is to admit your own ignorance. Then learn about God's omniscience. Under ordinary circumstances, we are so mixed up we have no more sense or strength than a worm trying to burrow through pavement. Without God, we are foolish; with Him, we can be exceedingly wise. Tap into God's wisdom.

Learn the difference between God's nature and ours. God is all-powerful; we are weak. God is beautiful; we are ugly. God is truth and honesty; we are deceitful and dishonest. God is wise; we are foolish. God is faithful; we are unfaithful. God is full of love; we are full of hate.

When you get a clear picture of what humans are like, be thankful. Then do the smart thing. Turn yourself over to your Creator. He holds His hands out to you. They're big enough for you to jump into. His hands will protect you, warm you, heal you. Listen for His voice; it will warn you, encourage you, teach you.

Because God loves us He wants us to live in strength, not weakness. He wants us to live, not die, and He wanted it so strongly that He sent His perfect Son, Jesus Christ, to sinful earth to die a painful death at the hands of an angry mob. We don't have to settle for a miserable life and a hopeless death. Through a process called redemption, we can have an abundant life, and death becomes a doorway through which we enter eternal life.

And furthermore, God wants to rescue us from the realms of the ordinary and make us more and more like Him through a process called sanctification.

Rejoice! Join the apostle Peter as he quotes David: "I was assured in advance of my Lord's abiding presence; He is right beside me to keep me from being knocked out. That's why my heart sings out and my tongue shouts for joy. And even more, my whole body will be vibrant with hope; Because you will not abandon my life to the grave, nor give your 'divine spark' to the despair of death. You have let me in on life's secrets; With your presence you will make me unspeakably happy."[1]

There are lots of ways to live. Many work for a while, but God's way is the only one that works for eternity.

Get into it—all the way in.

[1]Acts 2:25–28, quoting Psalm 16:8–11, as translated by Clarence Jordan, *The Cotton Patch Version of Luke and Acts* (New York: Association Press, 1969).

Recommended Reading

Developing Self-Esteem

Berry, J. *Can You Love Yourself?* Ventura, CA: Regal Books, 1978.

Narramore, S. B. *You're Someone Special.* Grand Rapids: Zondervan Publishing House, 1978.

Trobisch, W. *Love Yourself: Self-Acceptance and Depression.* Downers Grove, IL: InterVarsity Press, 1976.

Wagner, M. E. *Put It All Together: Developing Inner Security.* Grand Rapids: Zondervan Publishing House, 1974.

———. *The Sensation of Being Somebody: Building an Adequate Self-Concept.* Grand Rapids: Zondervan Publishing House, 1975.

Healing Emotional Wounds

Lawrence, R. *Christian Healing Rediscovered.* Downers Grove, IL: InterVarsity Press, 1980.

Scanlon, M. *Inner Healing: Ministering to the Human Spirit Through the Power of Prayer.* New York: Paulist Press, 1974.

Seamands, D. A. *Healing for Damaged Emotions.* Wheaton, IL: Victor Books, 1981.

———. *Putting Away Childish Things.* Wheaton, IL: Victor Books, 1982.

Walters, R. P. *Forgive and Be Free: Healing the Wounds of Past and Present.* Grand Rapids: Zondervan Publishing House, 1983.